ABANDONED
ON THE PLAINS

Tony Worobiec (signature)

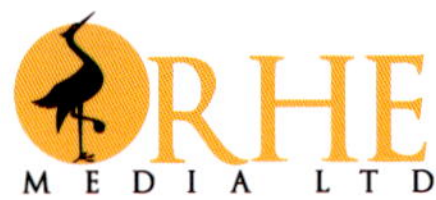

RHE
MEDIA LTD

ABANDONED ON THE PLAINS

FRAGMENTS OF THE AMERICAN DREAM

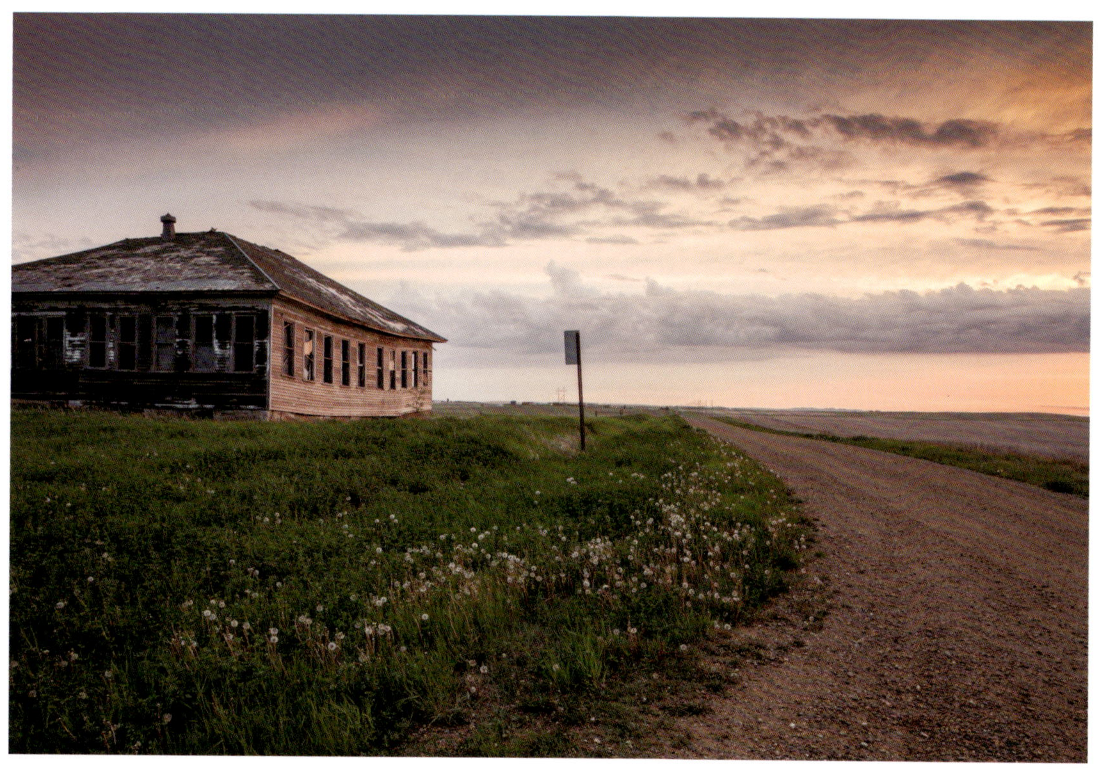

TONY & EVA WOROBIEC

INTRODUCTION

Drive along a quiet road anywhere on the High Plains and you are likely to see deserted farms and homesteads scattered along the way. Land in this part of America is cheap, generally because of the relative lack of employment opportunities, so if someone decides to abandon a property, it has little or no value. The reasons for people leaving are varied, but usually it was just an elderly person or couple who tired of living such an isolated existence. In many cases, because they had no children, or because their children had moved away, when they died there was nobody to take over. Similarly, many decided as they got older to move into sheltered housing; as a consequence the house or farm became redundant. In some areas, the extent of the abandonment shocked us; while we could understand the odd farm being deserted, it was not uncommon to stumble upon whole towns that had virtually disappeared within just a generation or two.

The High Plains stretch from Texas in the south to the Canadian border in the north, embracing parts of Oklahoma, Kansas, Colorado, Nebraska, South Dakota, North Dakota and eastern Montana. They have over decades supported a precarious form of agriculture; to the east where rainfall is more reliable, the farms are prosperous, while to the west the rugged Rocky Mountains form a natural barrier. Although there are areas of arable farming within the High Plains, much of the land is still given over to cattle-ranching: by its very nature, it is a sparsely populated region and it is not uncommon to travel 50 miles before reaching a sizable community. This is particularly noticeable the further north you travel.

With such a low population density when compared with Europe (and particularly with the UK), the value of land is low. If a property in Britain falls derelict, it is normally knocked down and replaced with something new. Small schools and churches never lie empty for long; often the function of these buildings changes as they are converted into community halls, gyms or even homes. By way of comparison, farms, homesteads, grain elevators, schools, and churches on the High Plains are simply abandoned, dependent on the prevailing economy of the time. We have been travelling to the States for 20 years, and never tire of investigating these strange and hauntingly beautiful places. Weathered and bleached under the unremitting cycle of hot summers and harsh winters, these iconic buildings stand isolated against the backcloth of the open plains. This is an area often referred to as "big sky country", a phrase which aptly describes how expansive and flat this region can be. It is an area which is also plagued by storms and tornadoes, which over a period of years take their inevitable toll on these fragile structures.

As Europeans travelling through America, one does need to be aware of certain cultural differences. For example, the laws relating to trespass are rigorously observed in the US, so if you do discover an abandoned building, it is not necessarily an invitation to enter. Whilst urbex photographers can 'disappear' into a busy city environment or, at worst, play cat-and-mouse with the occasional security guard, it is surprising how soon one can be spotted by a concerned farmer who seems to appear from nowhere. When we first started photographing deserted buildings in the 1990s, people were bemused then very interested in what we were doing. What made some residents more suspicious of strangers from about the mid-2000s was that several isolated buildings were used for the production of crystal meth, leading to crime and dangerous fires. During our recent visits, it has been noticeable how many of these abandoned properties have been securely locked or fenced in.

So just to be on the safe side, if there was a "no trespassing" sign posted, we observed it, no matter how isolated the building appeared to be. However, when access was no problem, we were often astonished by how well preserved some of the interiors were. Disturbed only by the odd racoon seeking shelter from the harshness of winter, many of the rooms appear much as they did when they were abandoned, possibly decades before. When entering what had been someone's home, it was important to remain respectful and while we tried not to move anything, we would look for those scraps of detail that hinted at what life was like those many years ago. Largely undisturbed, these interiors serve as time capsules on a period and culture neither of us had experienced. While our primary purpose is to photograph, an engagement with recent history certainly helps to place what we were witnessing within a broader context; old newspapers were particularly useful in this respect. Often simple things we might easily have overlooked, such as a calendar, an accounts book, a discarded letter or an old school journal helped to fill in the missing details.

There is of course an aesthetic dimension to this; in common with many photographers, we were drawn to the strangely illusive beauty one often finds in decay. With the advent of Photoshop, some opt for image-altering filters in order to artificially reproduce the process of ageing.
By photographing fading parchments or flaking bits of masonry and layering these with the original image, a shallow and insincere illusion of ageing can be created. We always sought to capture "the real thing", recognising that the gradual process of ageing produces its own unique testament to history.

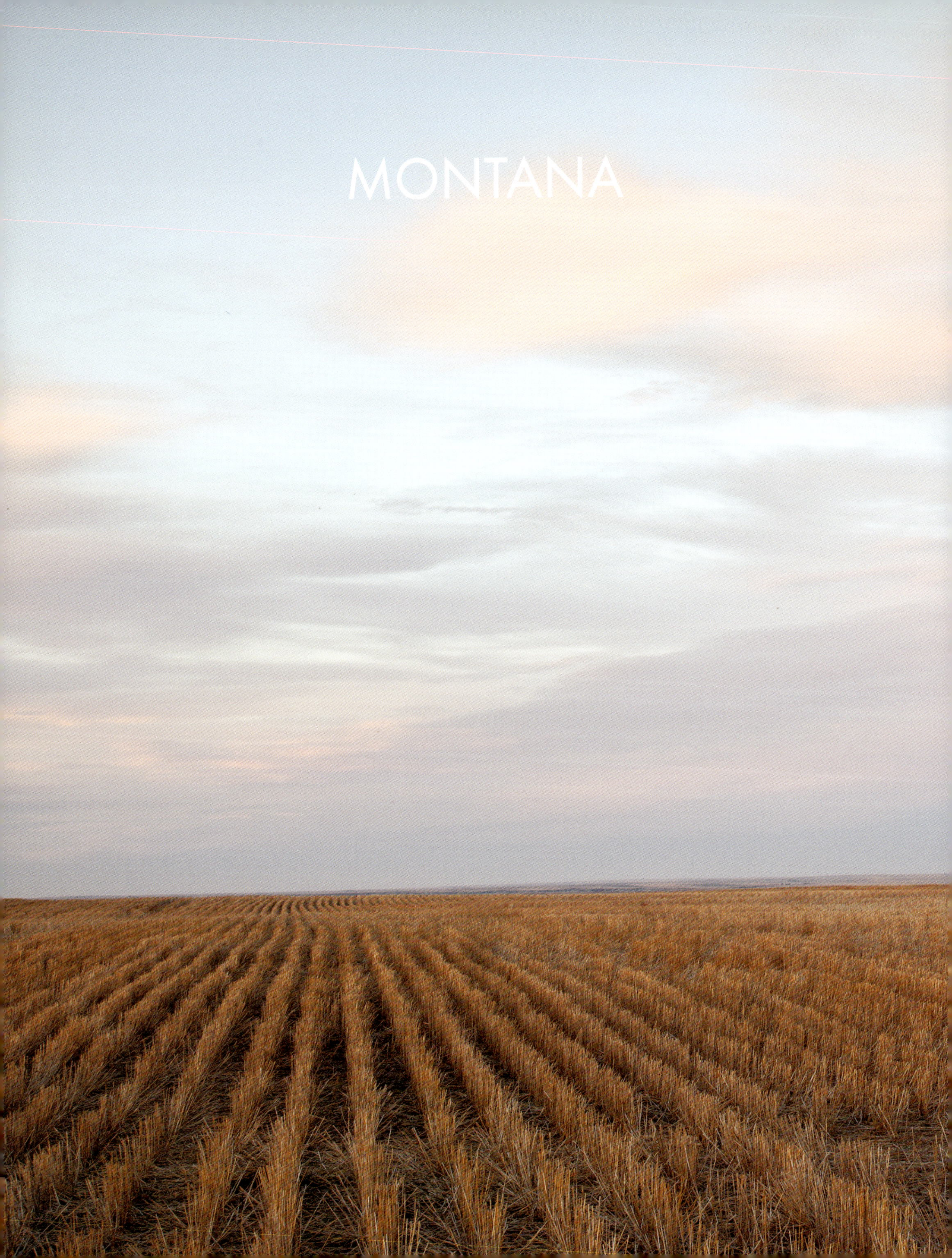
MONTANA

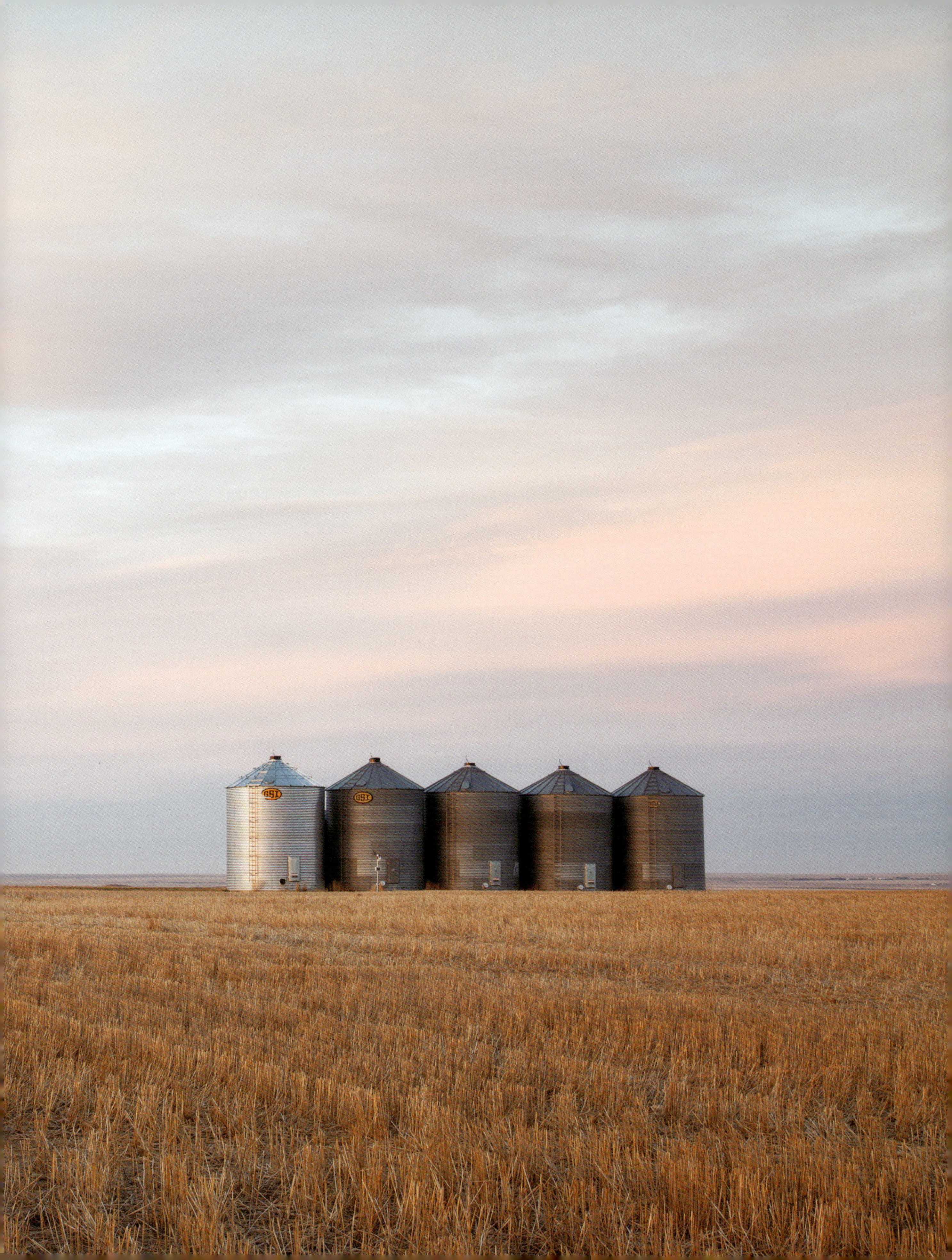

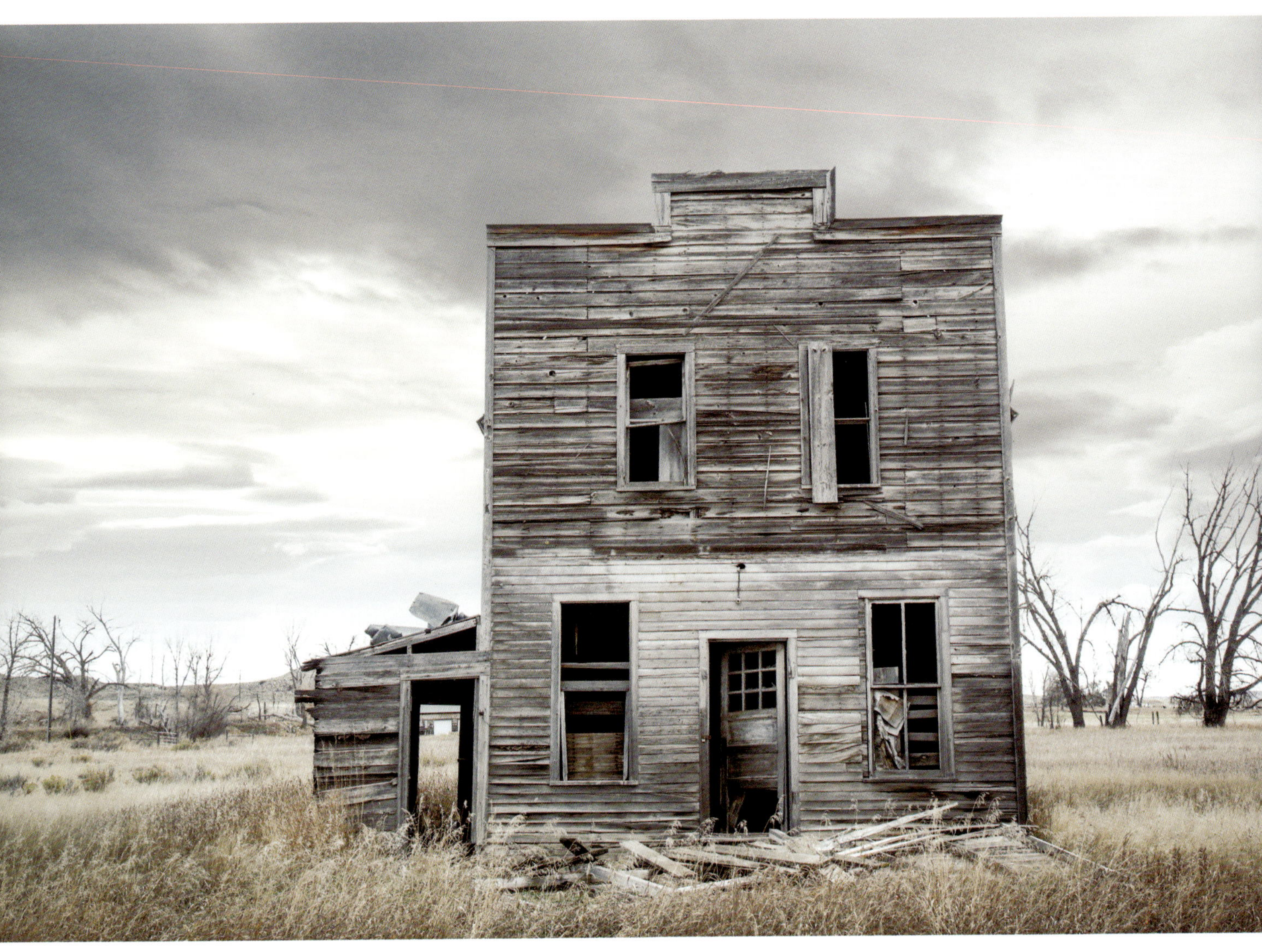

▲

Abandoned Hotel

Constructed entirely of timber, it is remarkable that
this fragile building is still standing. It also suggests
that this was once a town that had a commercial past.

▶

Bathroom cabinet, Grenora

It is astonishing what is often left behind. As we entered this
bathroom, we saw that the cabinet was still filled with medication
that was prescribed decades ago.

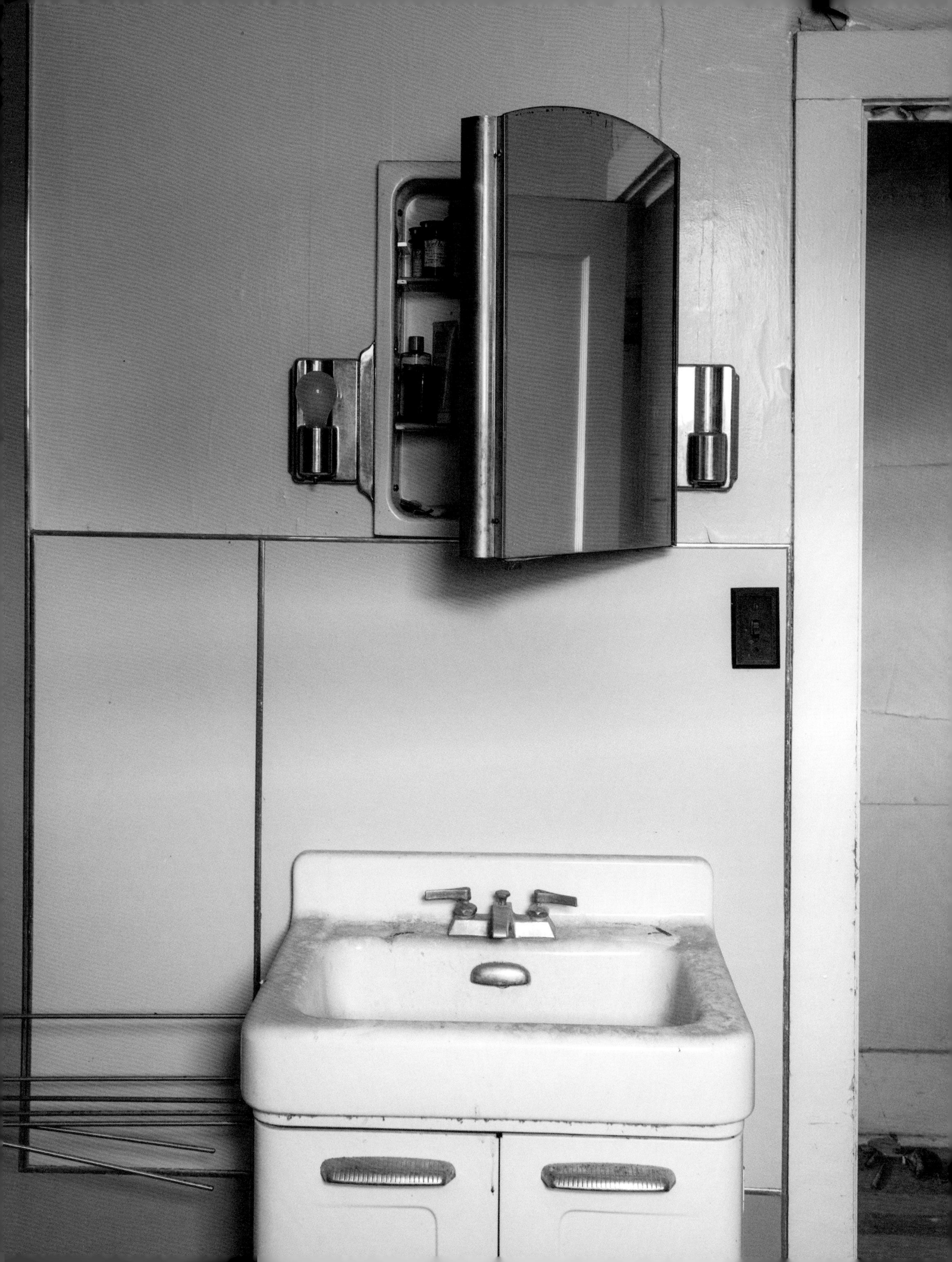

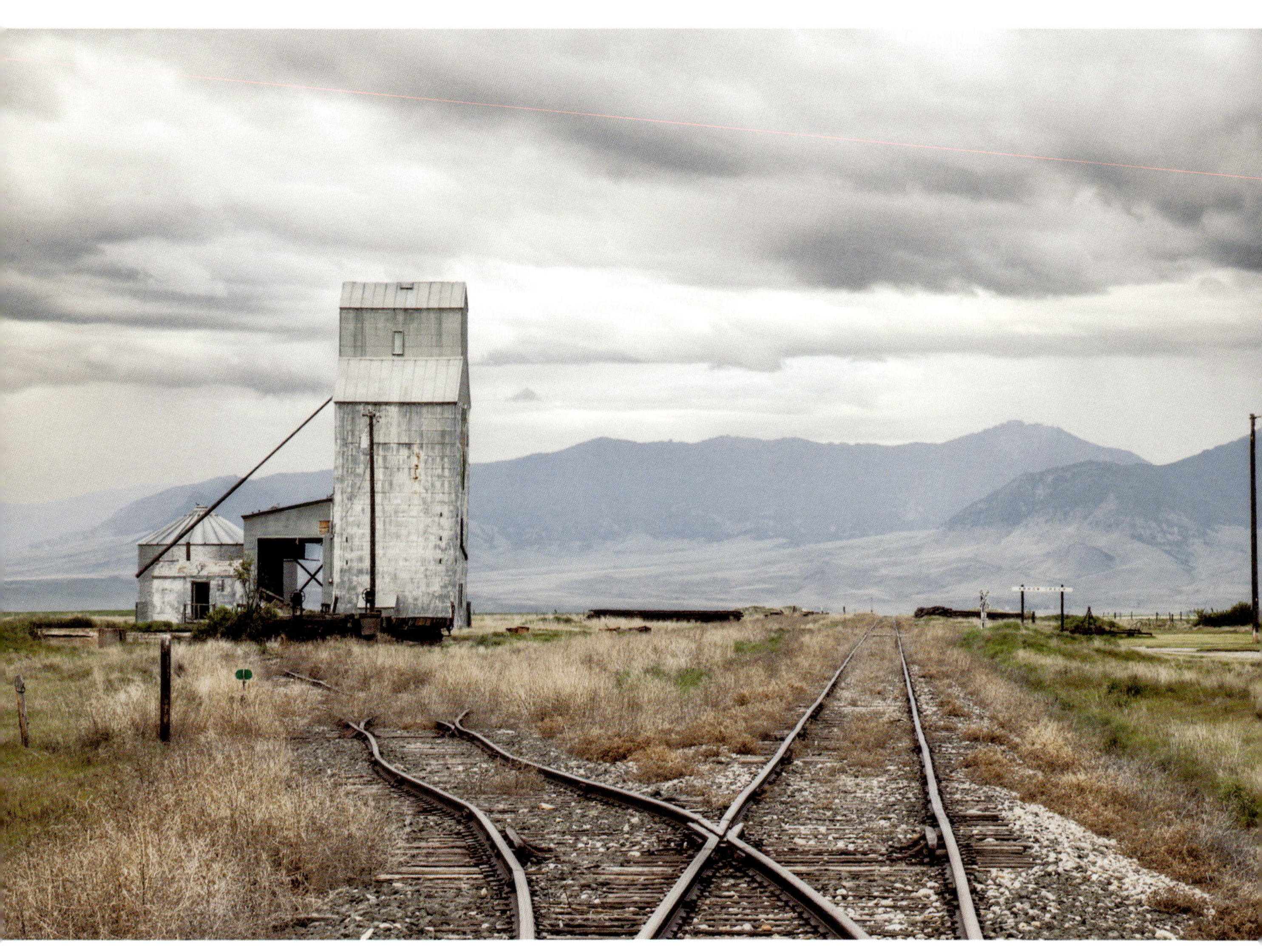

▲

Abandoned Grain Silo

*The railroad is the life-blood for agriculture on the High Plains, so
when it appears little used, it is a sure sign that the area generally
is in decline.*

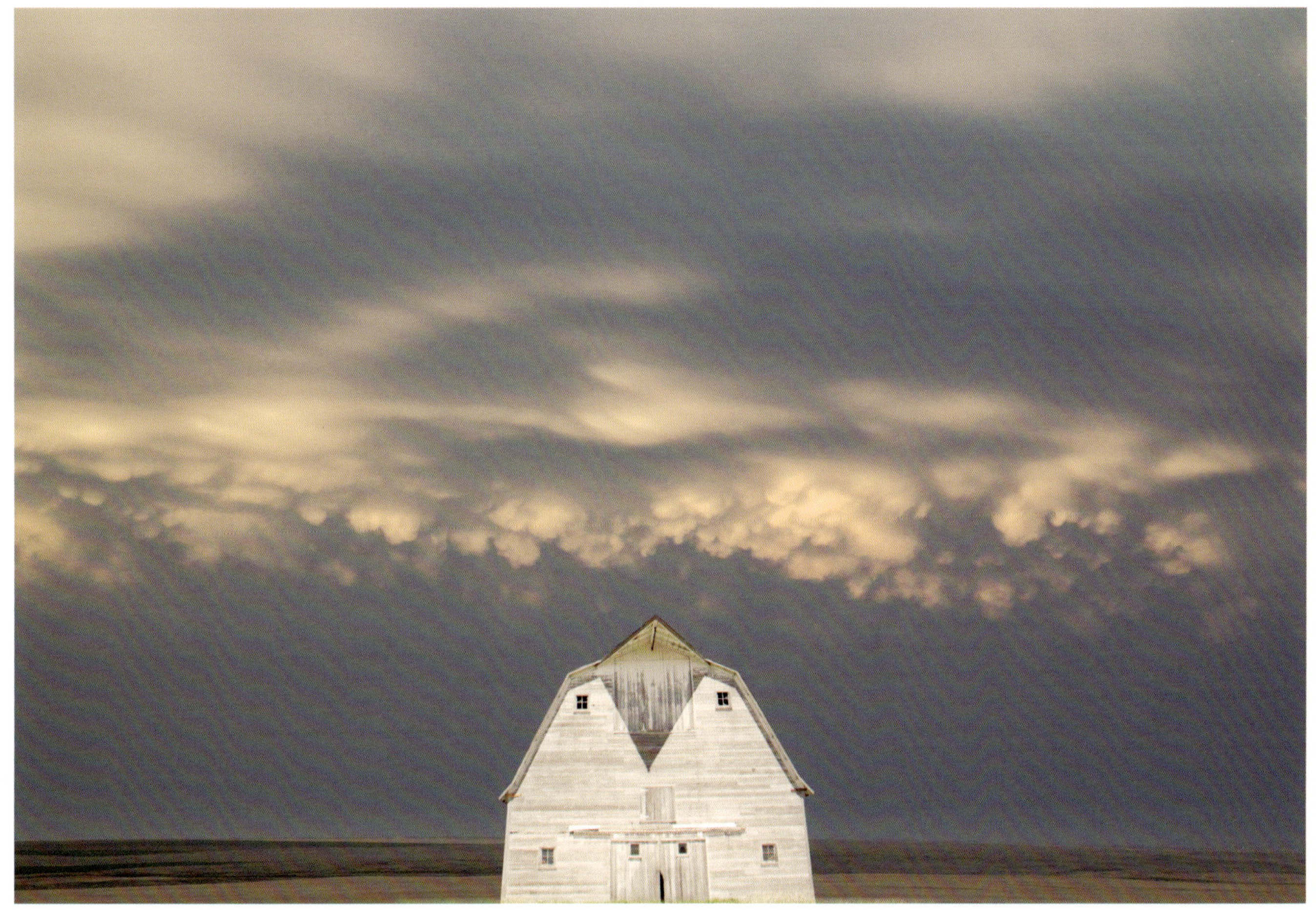

Barn under threatening sky

Photographed in late spring, we became accustomed to seeing these awesome mammatus cloud formations created by passing tornadoes, which blight this part of America at this time of year.

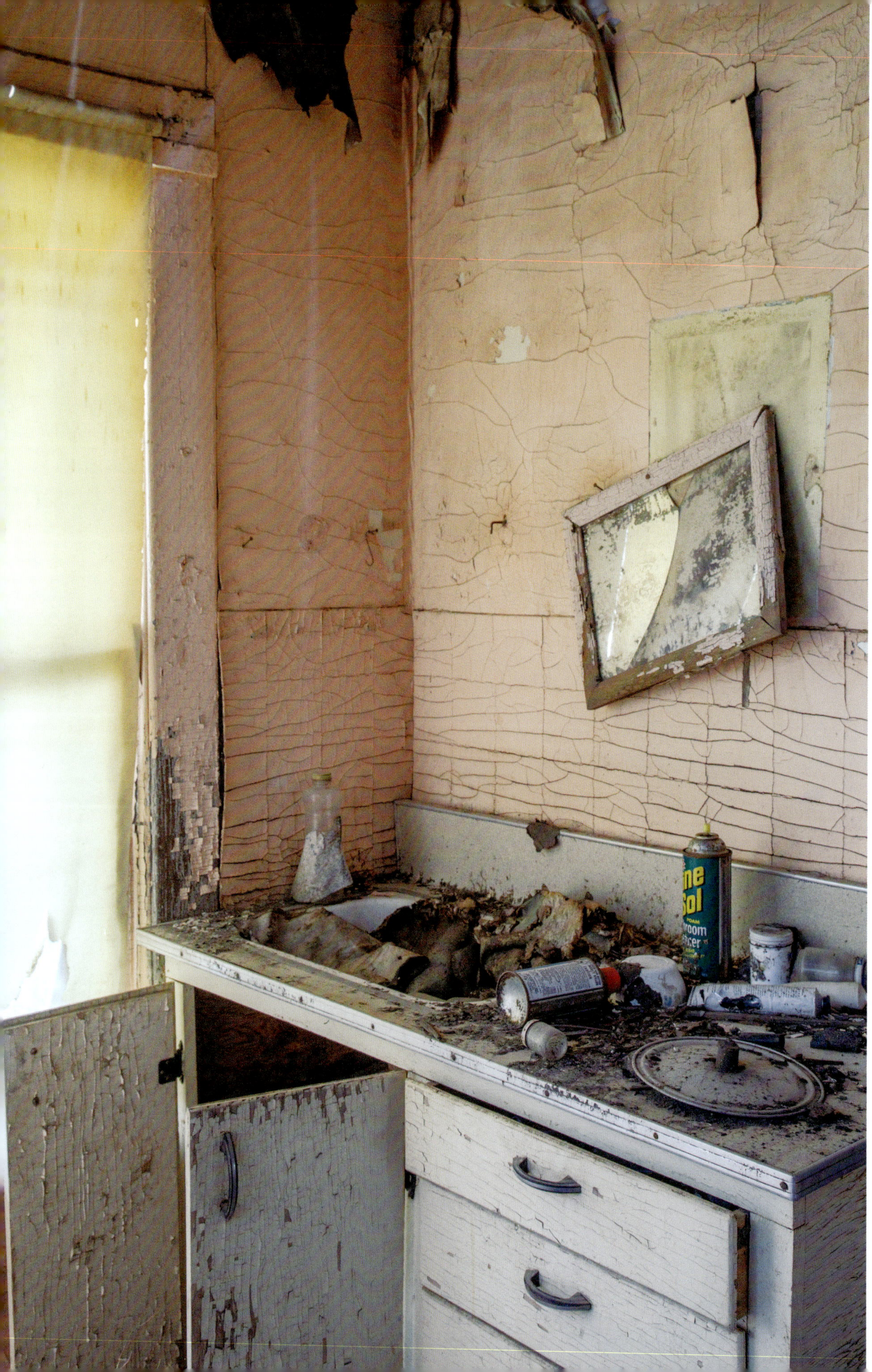

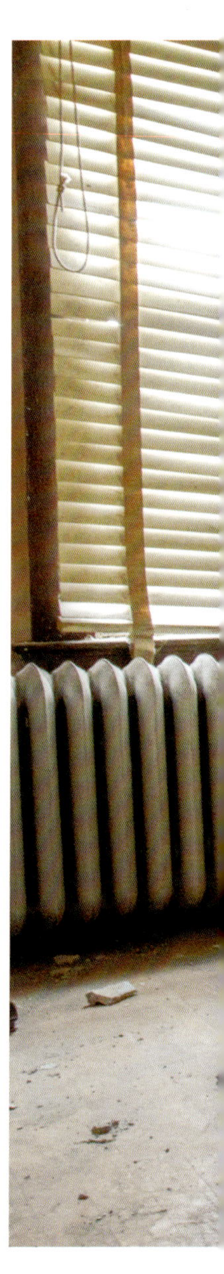

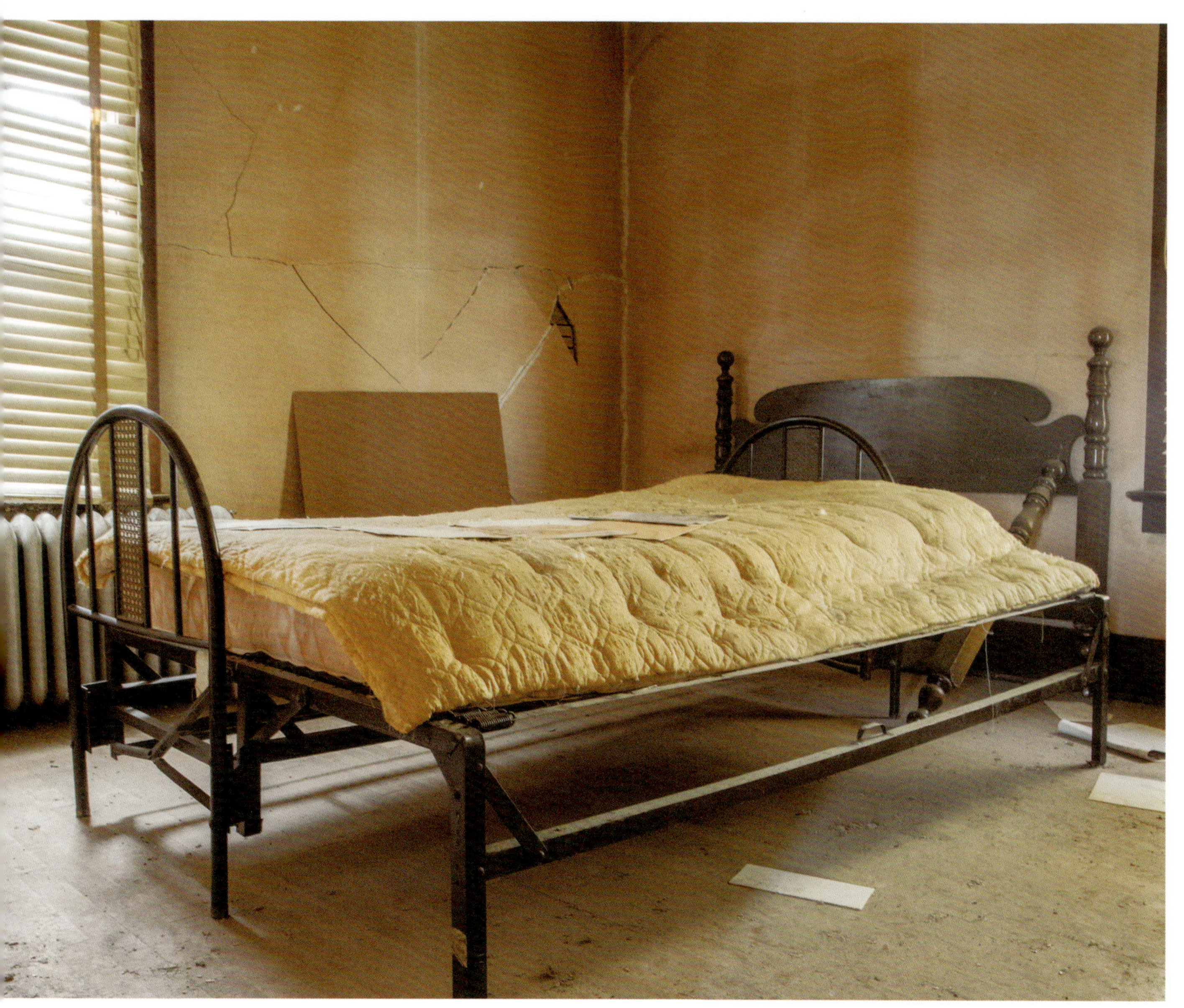

Bedroom, Rosebud County

When encountering a scene like this, it is often difficult to imagine that the owners have long since departed.

Interior near Devon

So many questions: was this house abandoned by a family in financial trouble or was the previous occupant an elderly person who had no close relatives?

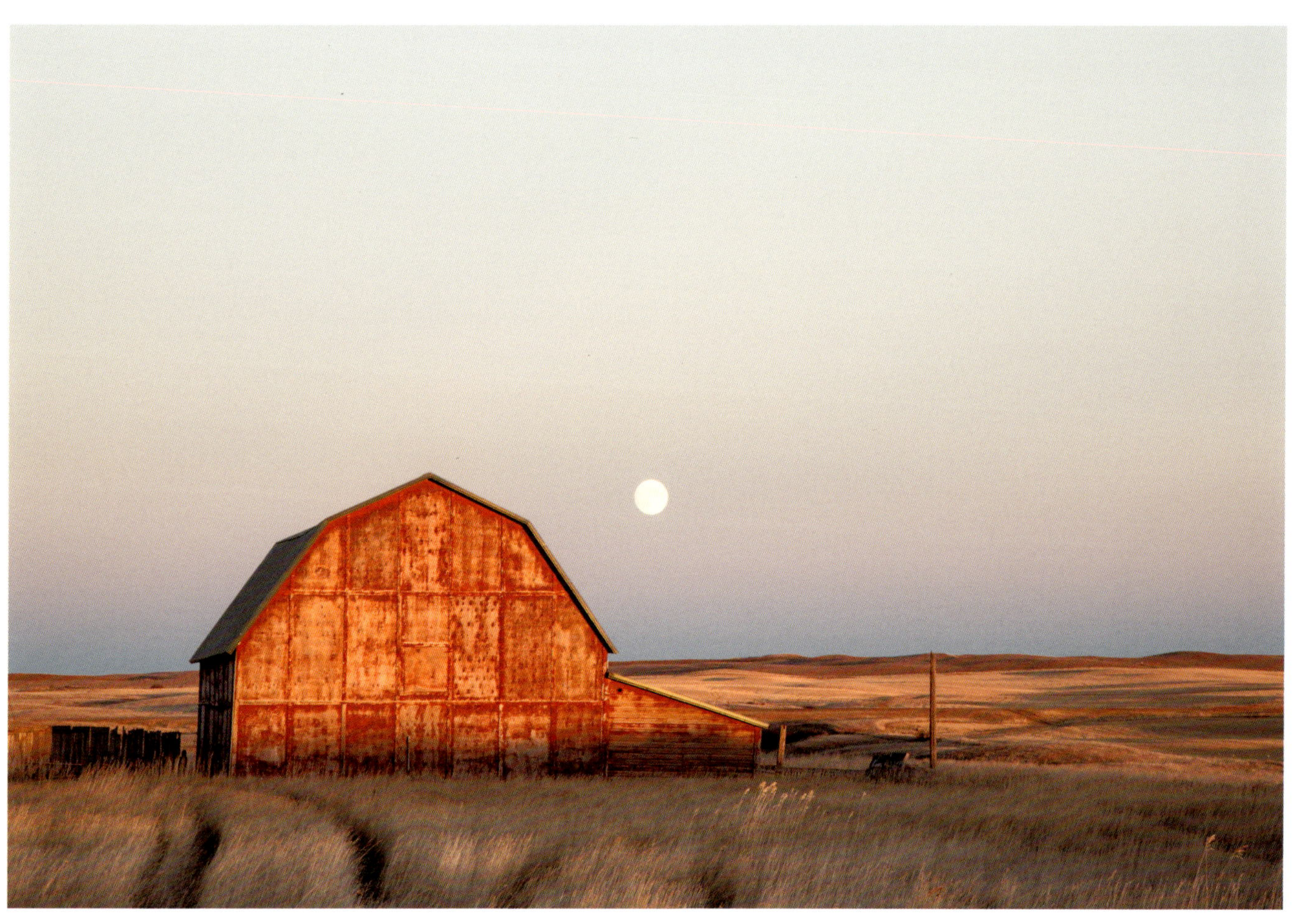

Red barn and moon, north of Plentywood

*Photographed just a few miles short of the Canadian border, it is
hard to imagine an area more remote than this.*

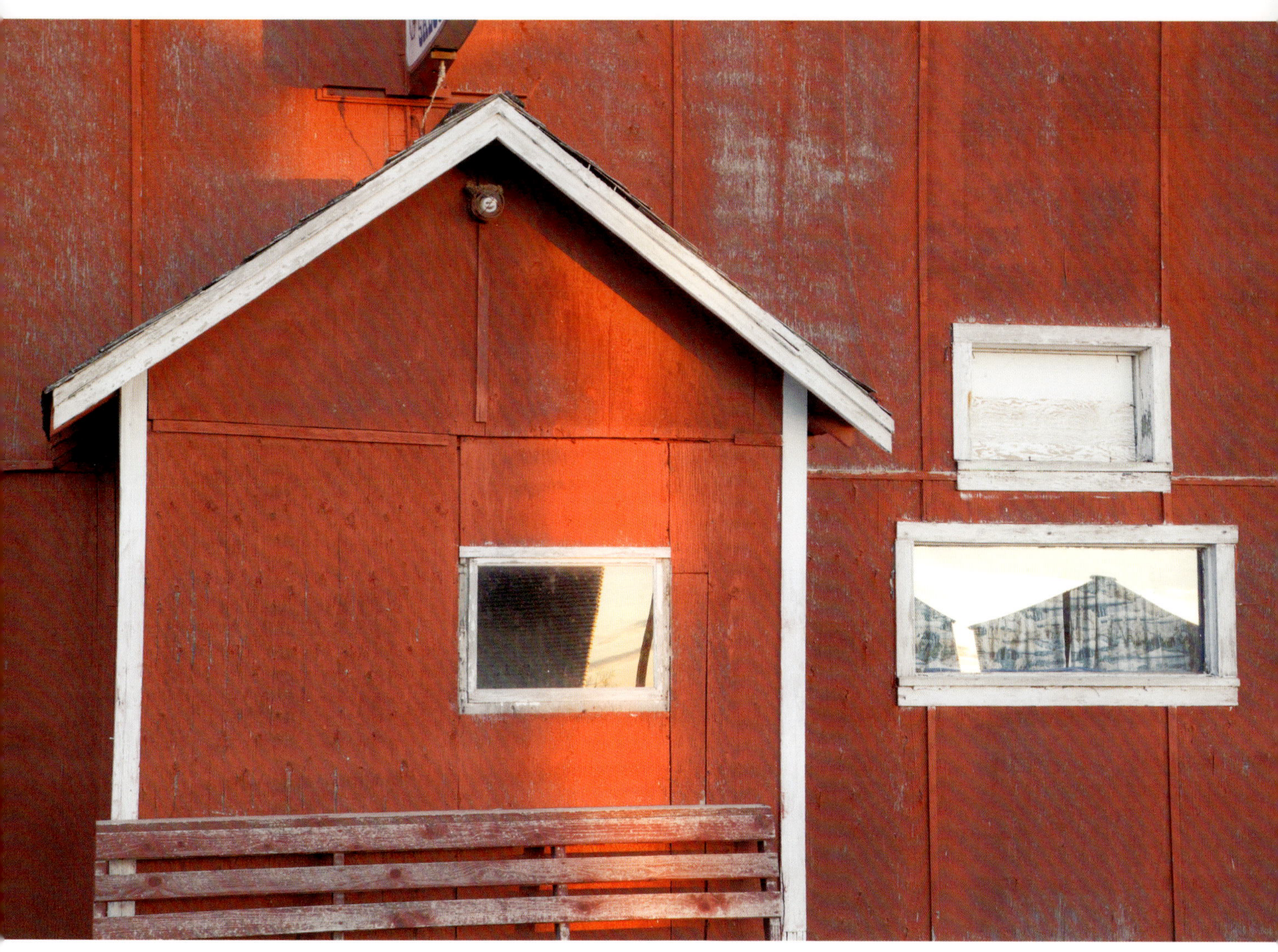

▲

Side of barn, Raymond

*This old barn appeared to have acquired a new lease of life as the
"Last Chance" saloon bar. The small community of Raymond is
situated about 9 miles south of the Canadian border.*

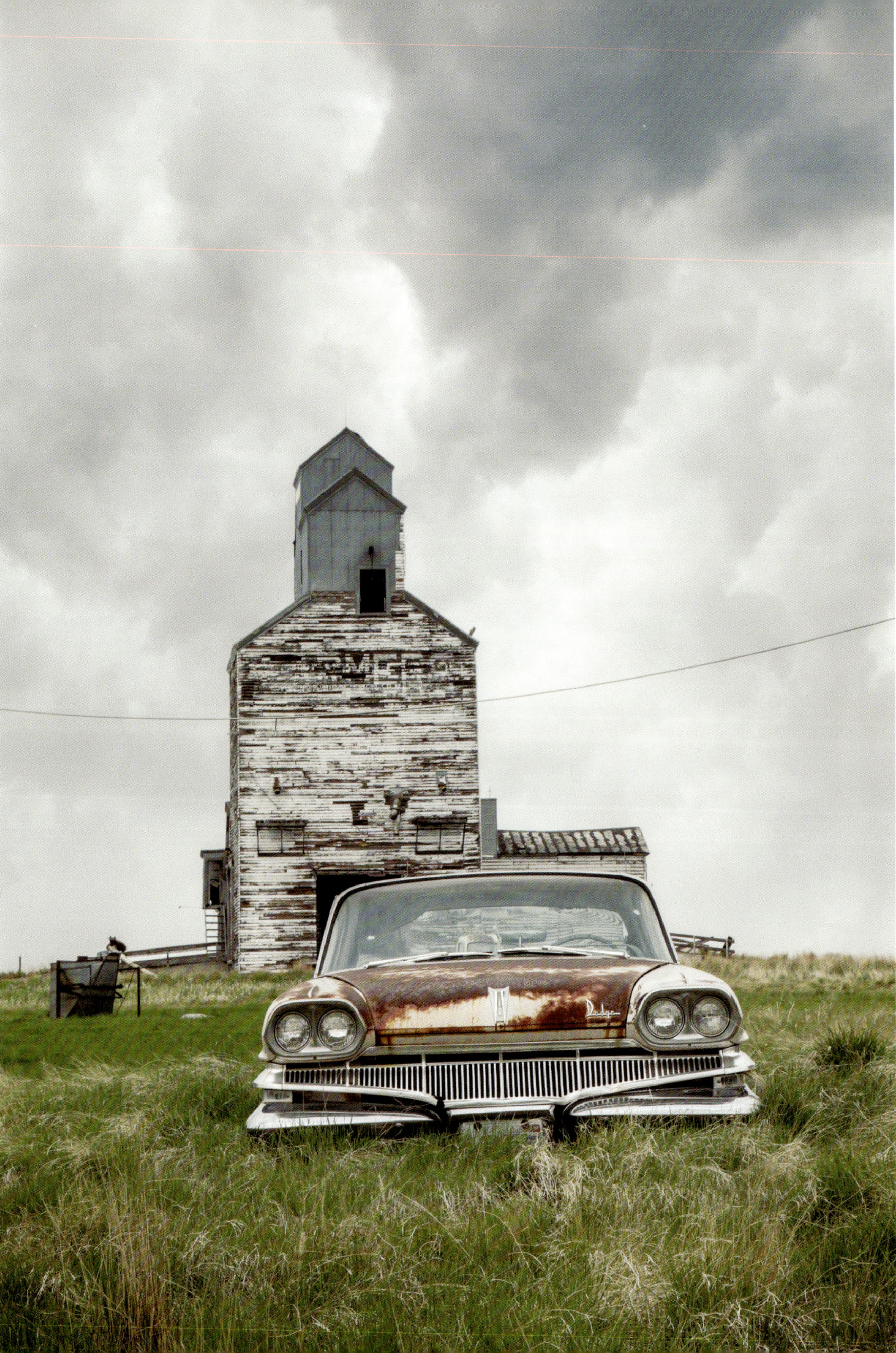

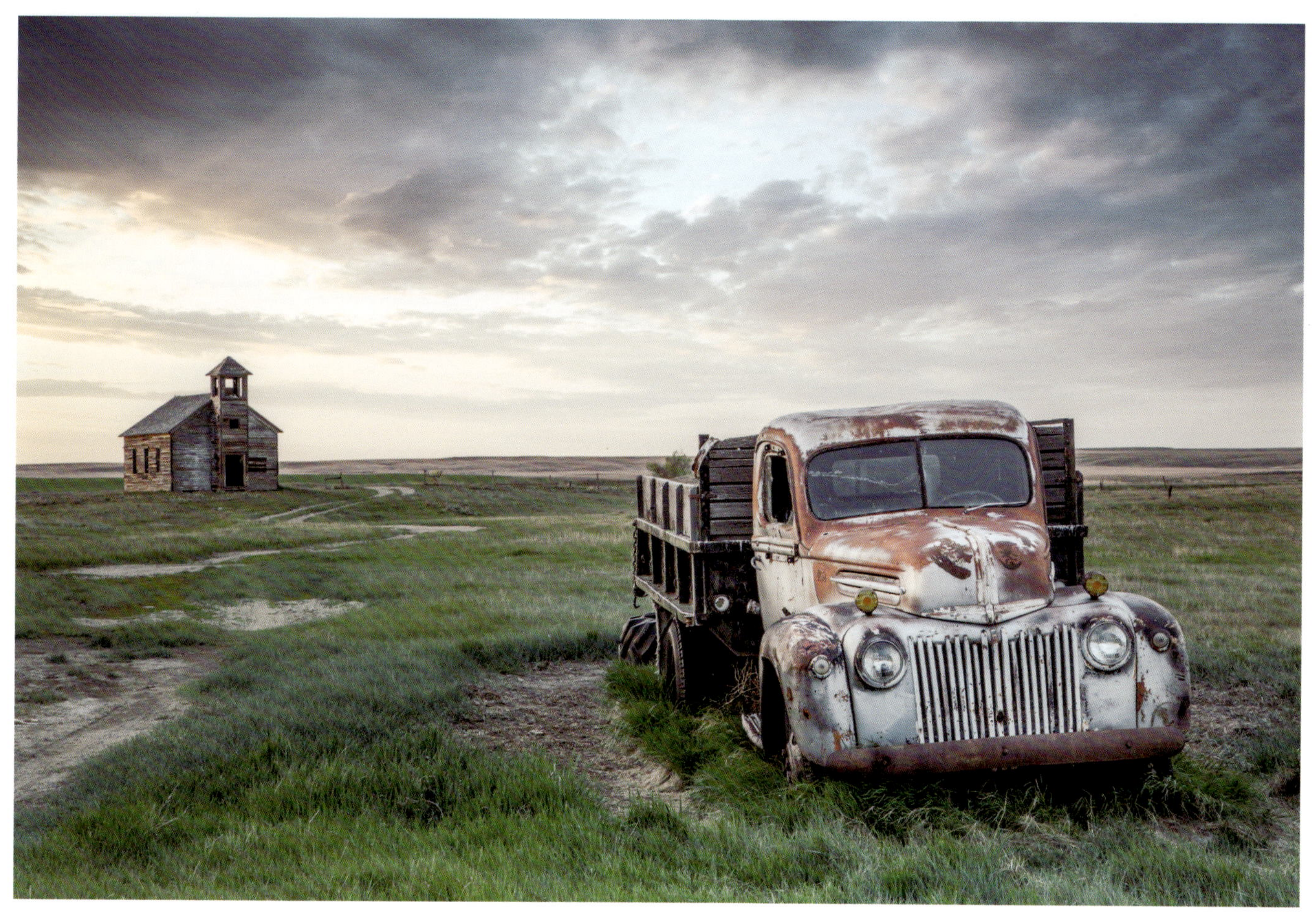

Ford truck and Cottonwood Church

*About 30 miles north of the town of Havre, this is another location
which straddles the Canadian border. One senses that this church
has been abandoned for many decades.*

Abandoned Dodge and elevator

*This community, only about 14 miles from the Canadian border,
used to be on a branch line of the Great Northern Railroad, but the
last trains went through here past the elevator in 2001.*

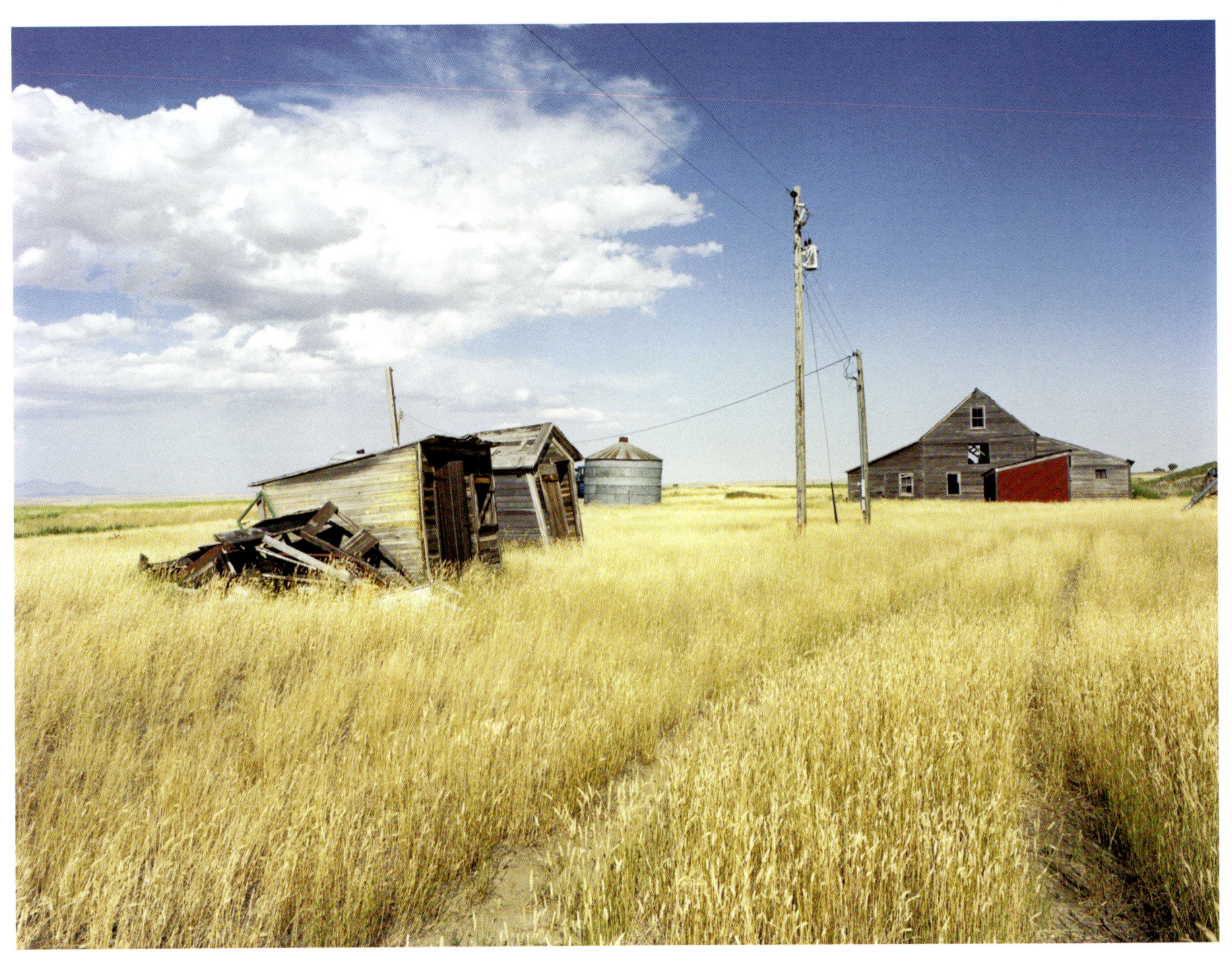

Abandoned farm, Dunkirk

Situated on the Hi-Line 10 miles east of Shelby, Dunkirk's population now numbers just a handful.

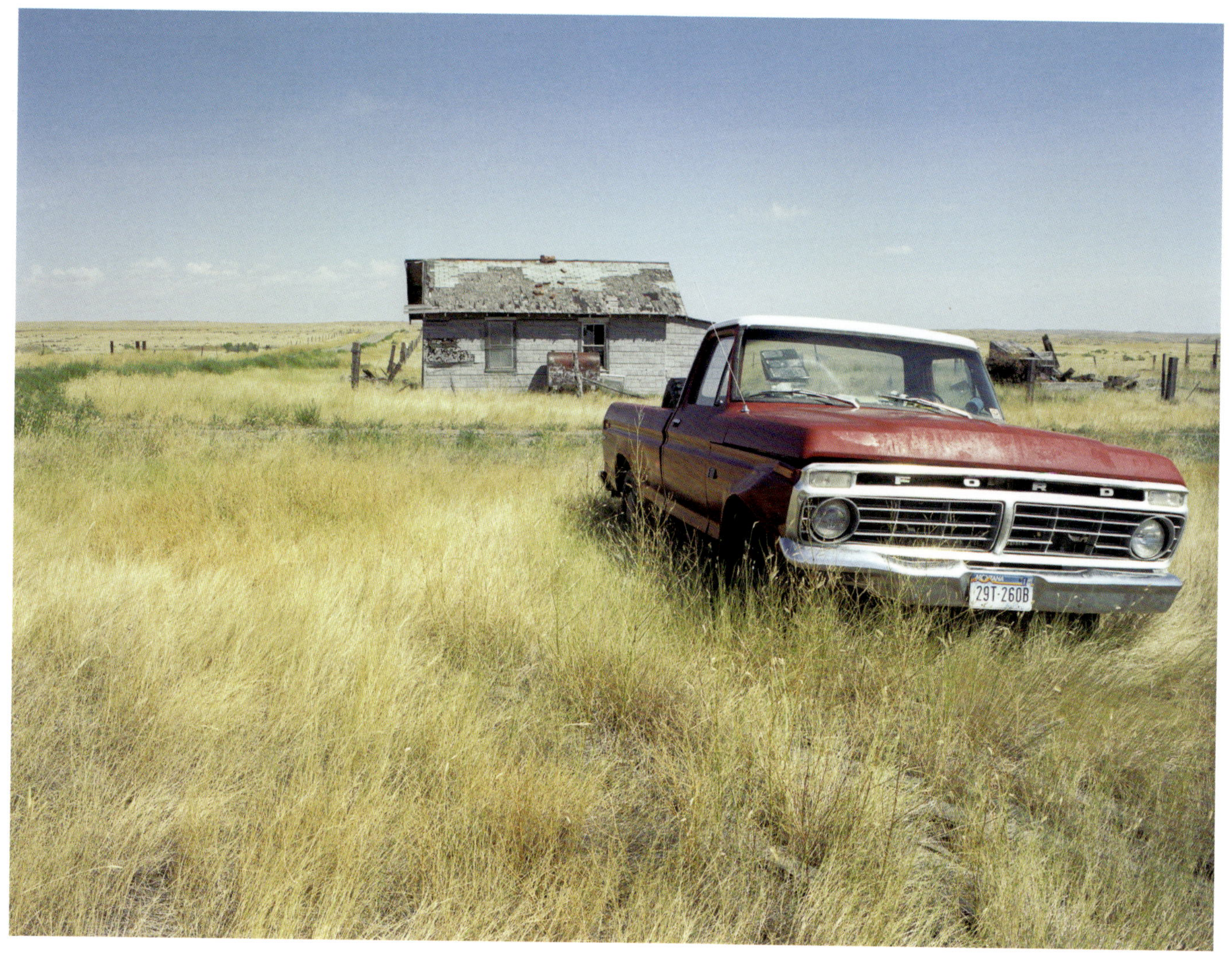

Abandoned homestead and pickup,
on Hwy 12 near Sumatra, Rosebud County

*One of several small communities which sprang up in the early
20th century along the now defunct Chicago, Milwaukee and St
Paul railway, Sumatra consists of a few houses and a post office.*

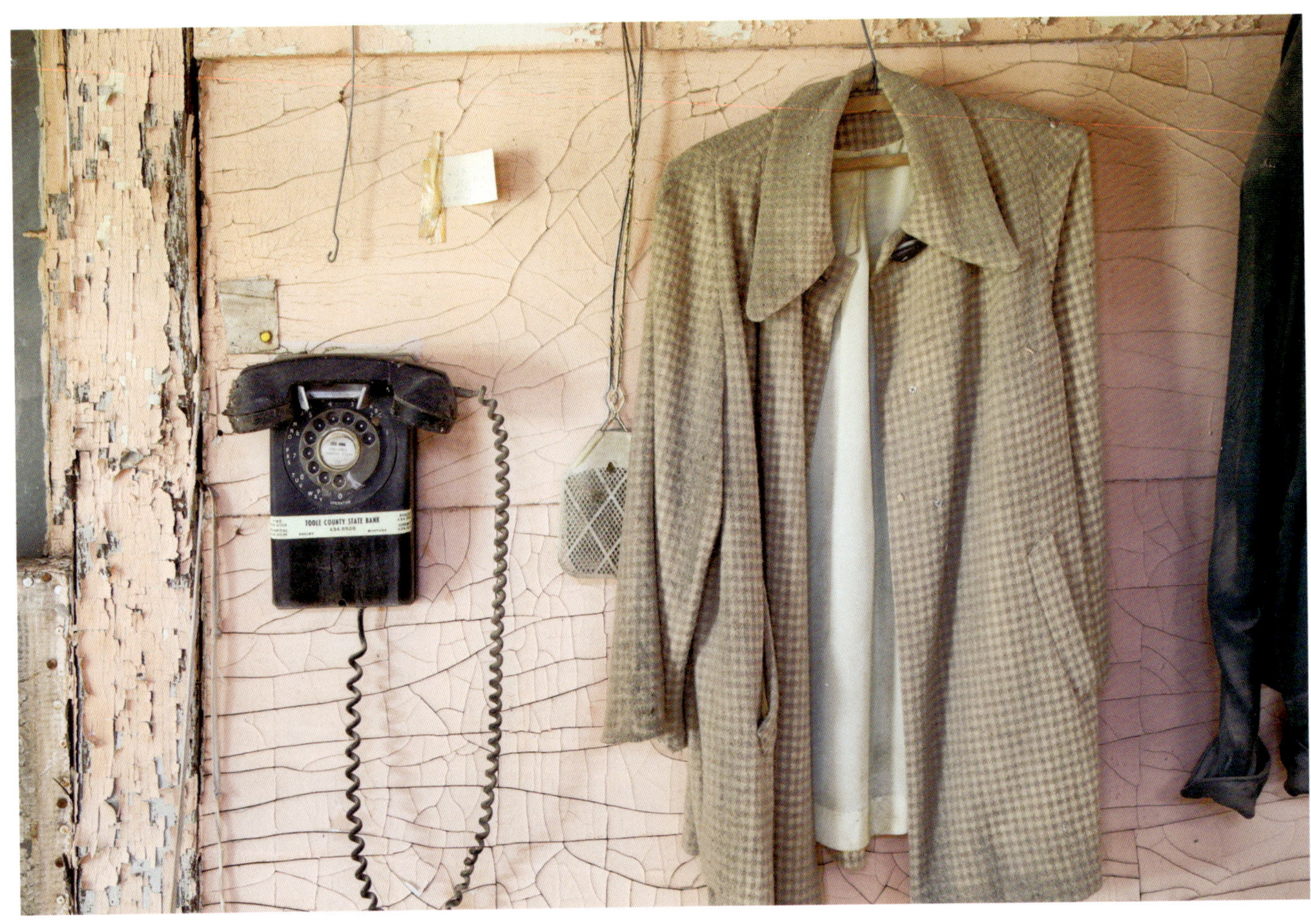

Coat and Telephone

*What makes this picture so remarkable is that we first took
it over 15 years ago; this interior appears to have remained
untouched in all that time.*

Interior with open door

*Only the mess on the floor from crumbling ceiling plaster
indicates that this property is no longer occupied.*

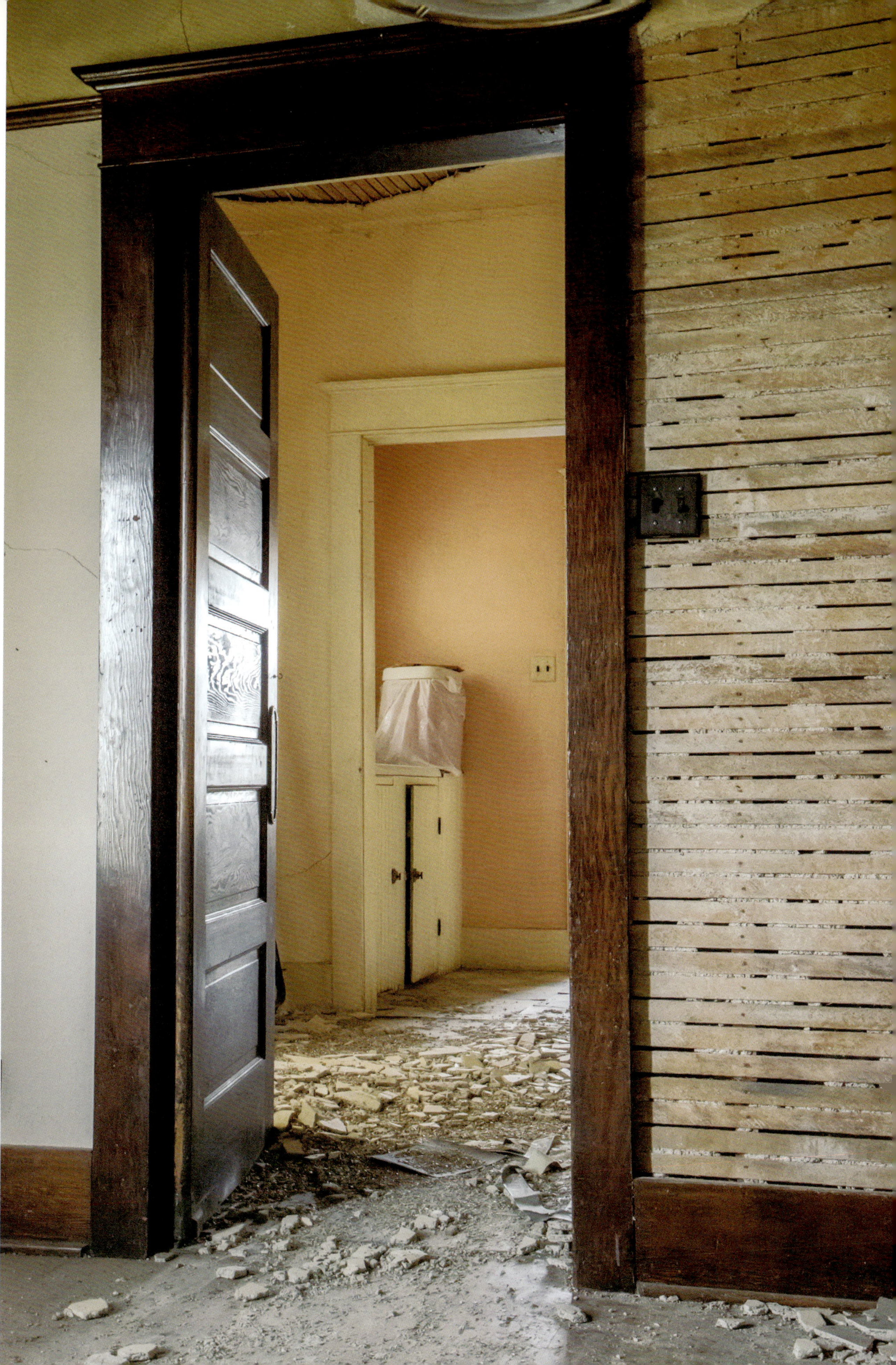

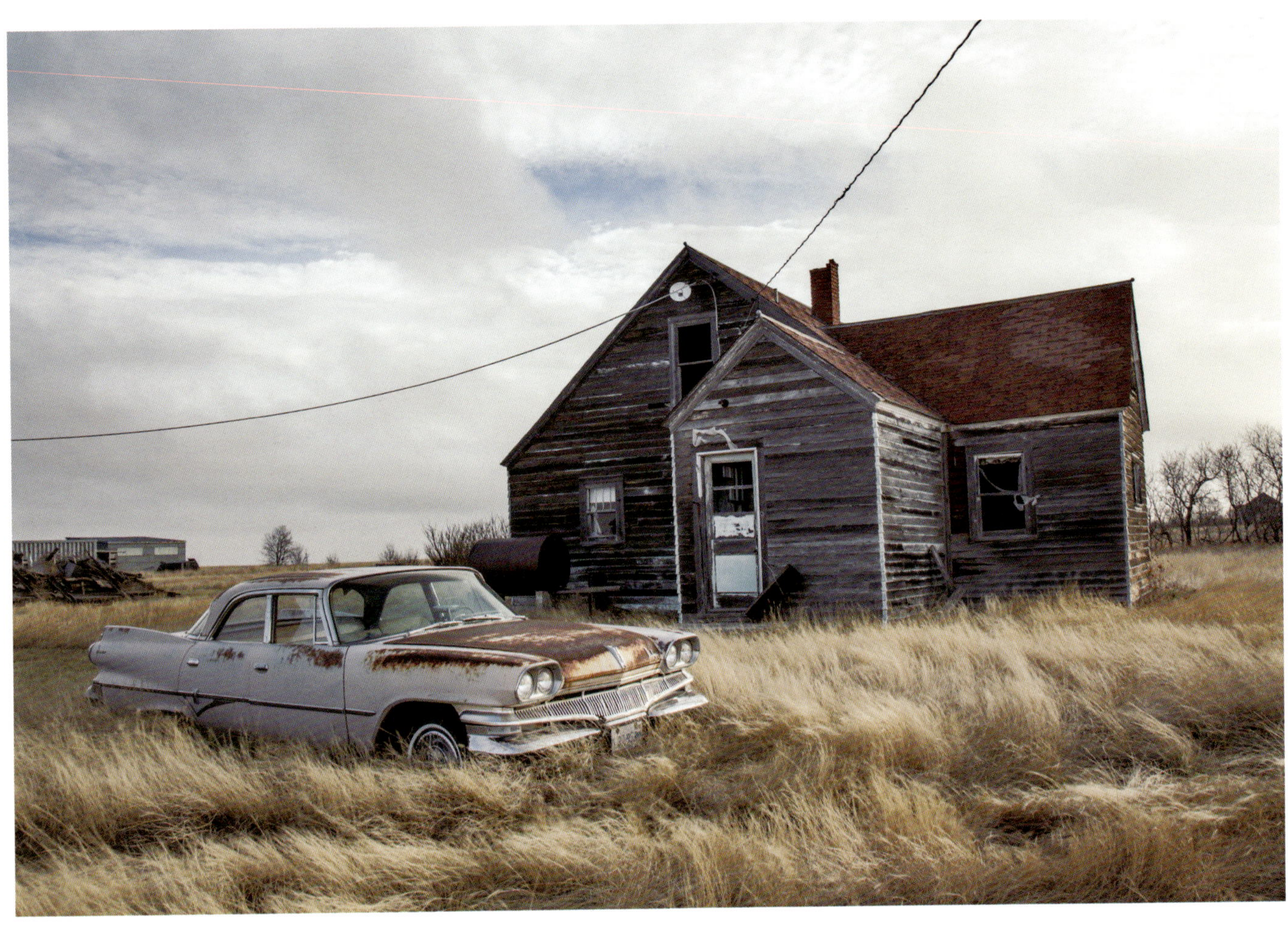

▲

Abandoned house, Daniels County

Probably due to its relative isolation in a quiet corner of northeast Montana, this vehicle and house have remained untouched for many years.

23

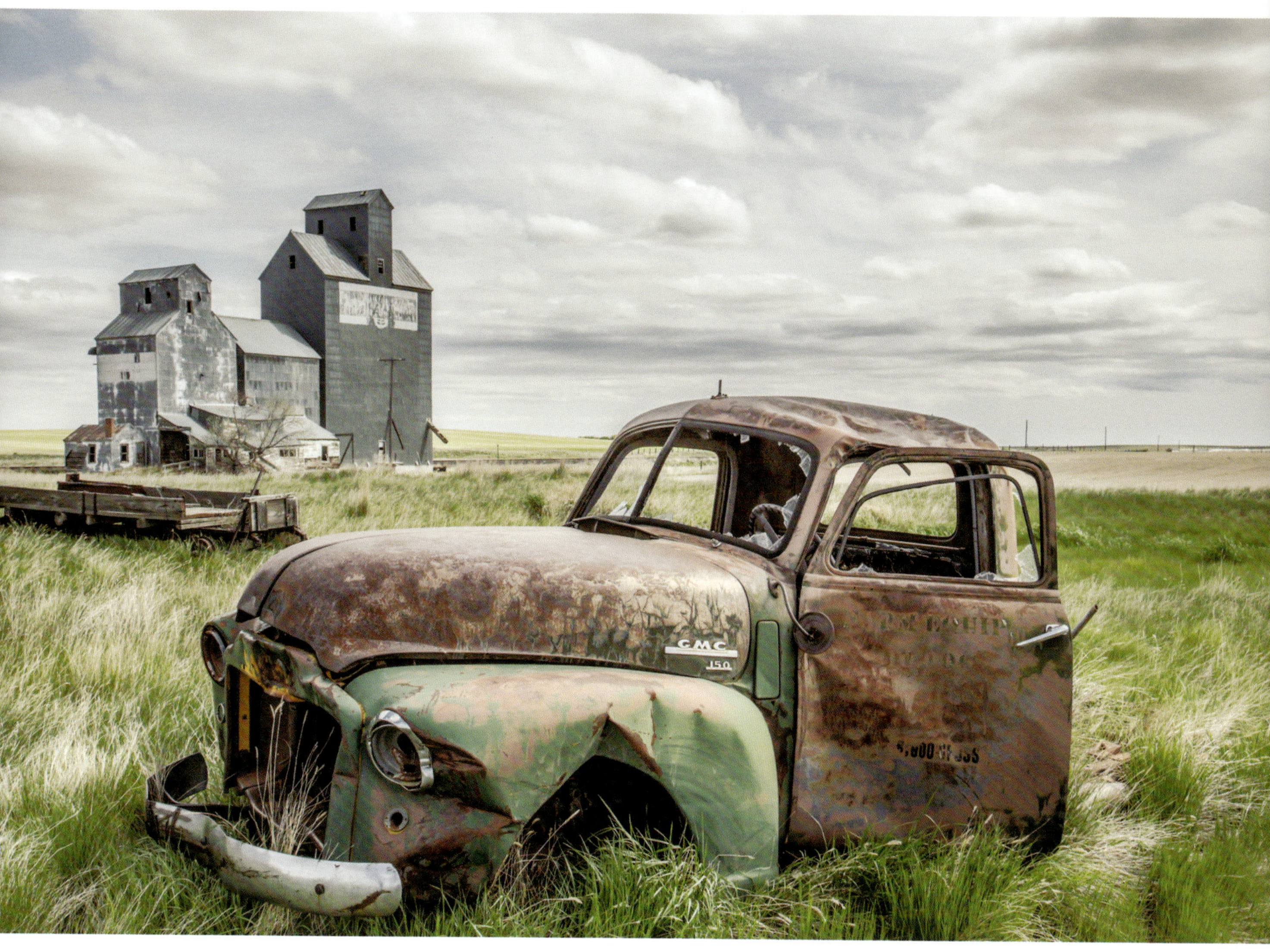

GMC Pick-up and elevators, Dunkirk

This is another location we had photographed many years previously and amazingly very little has changed. The population of Dunkirk has significantly reduced in recent decades.

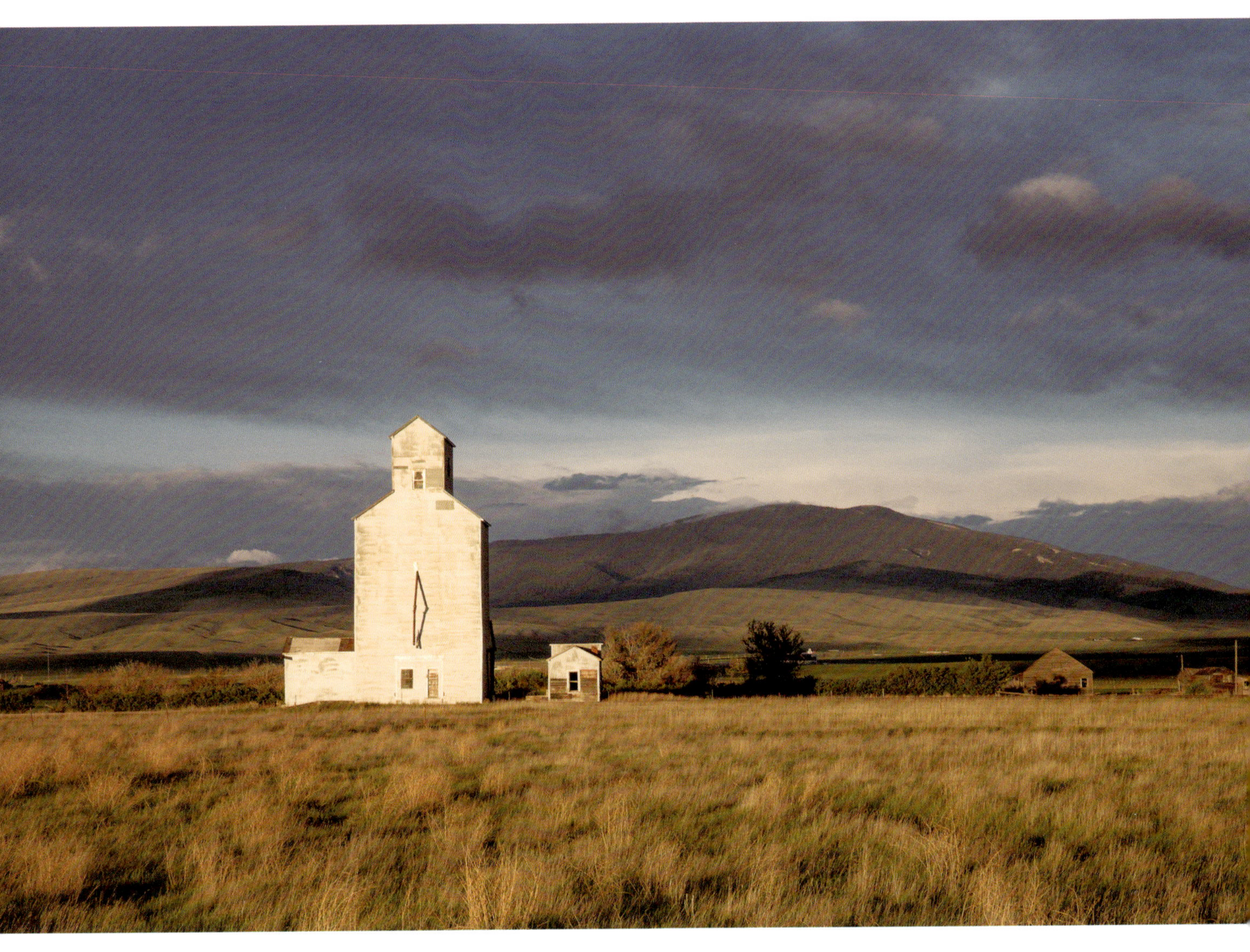

▲

Elevator, central Montana

Situated some 30 miles south of Lewistown, the derelict white grain elevator gleams in the evening sun against the Little Belt mountains.

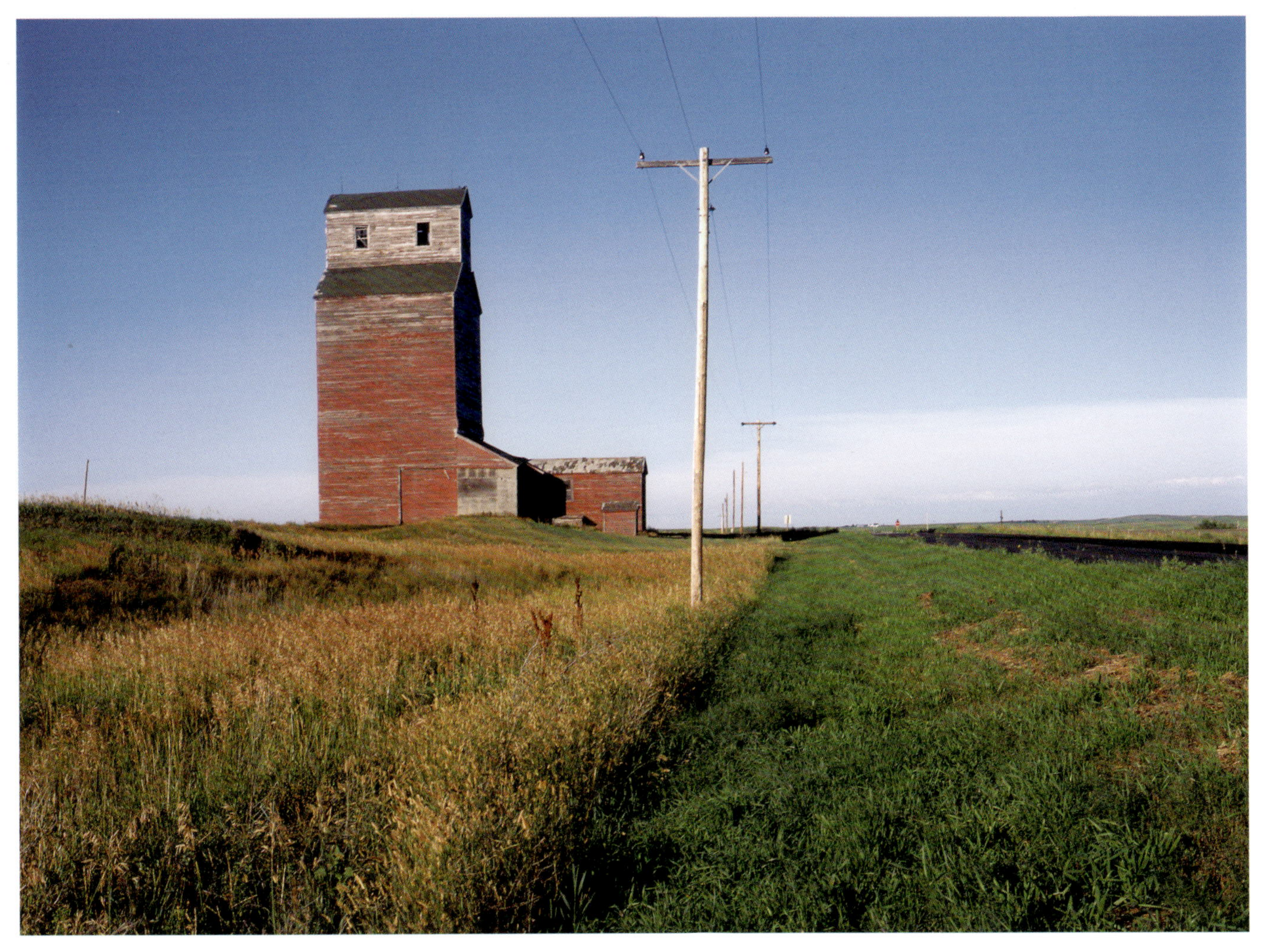

Red elevator near Raymond

*Very few of the original wooden grain elevators now remain, which
is a pity, as often their unique colours and shapes, seen from some
distance away, draw one towards their small communities.*

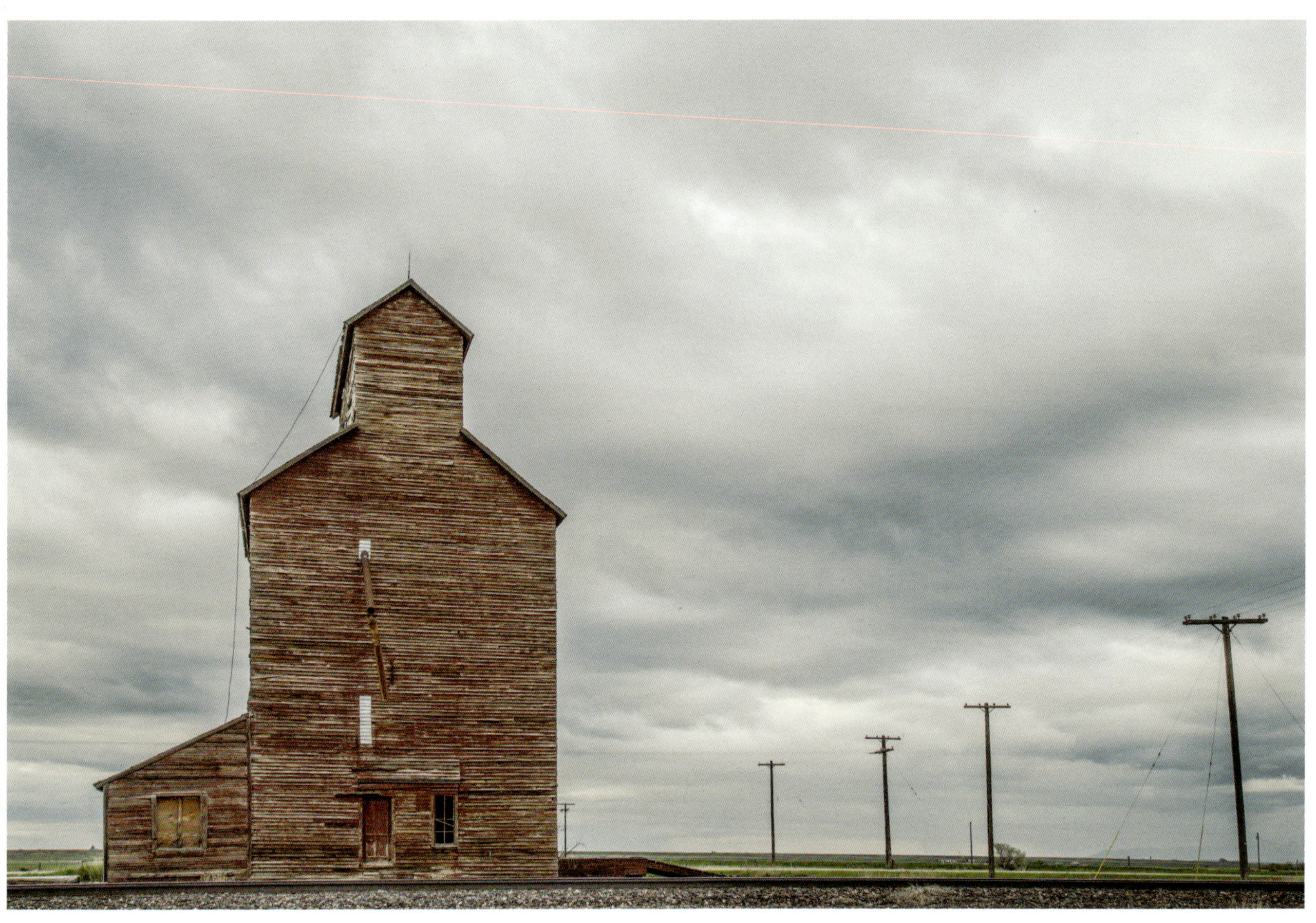

Red elevator, Moccasin

Located on the edge of town, the overwhelming majority of elevators were constructed next to the railway line.

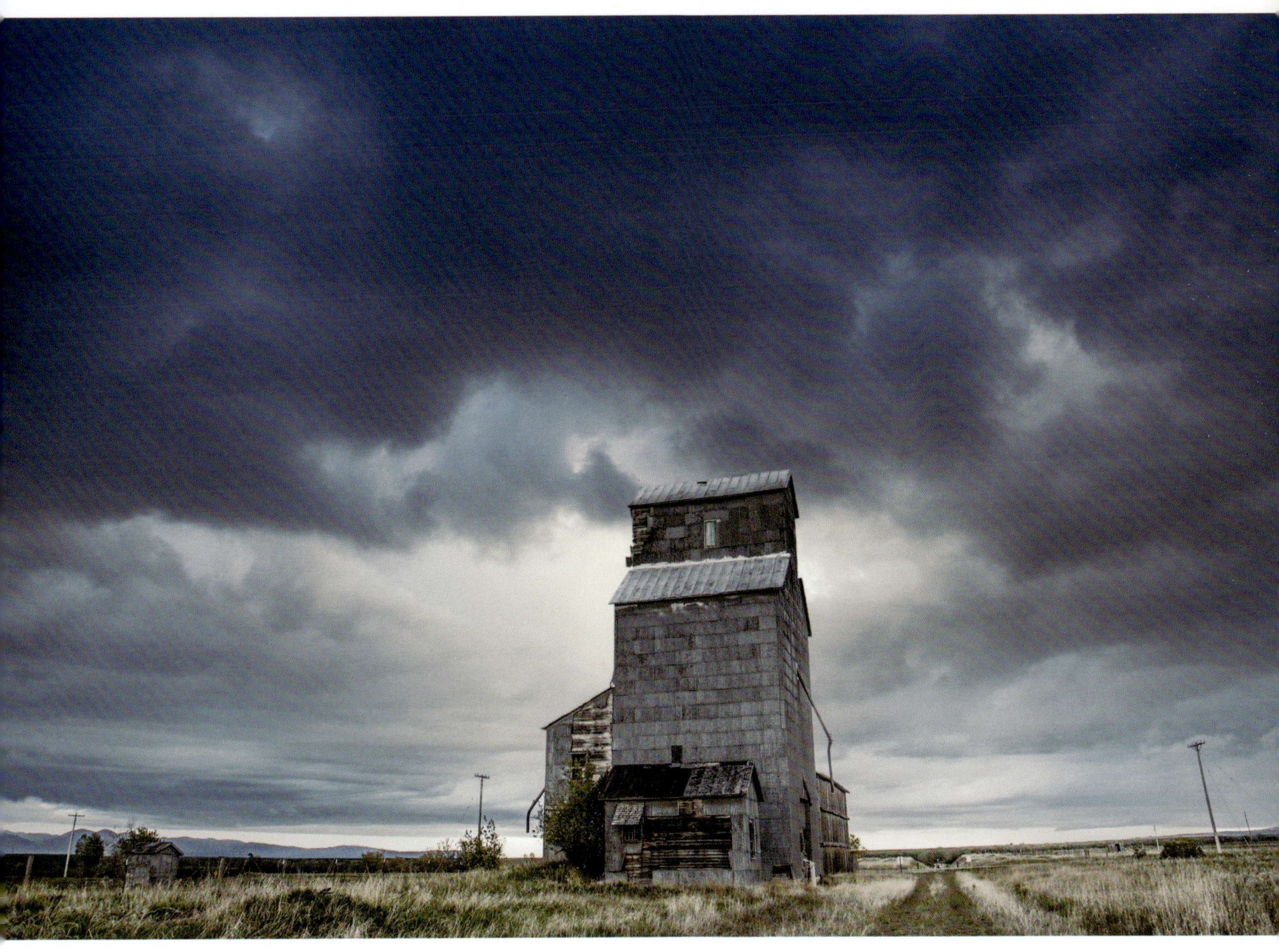

▲

Elevator, Glengarry, Montana

Storms and bad weather regularly batter buildings and large structures throughout the High Plains, which only adds to the difficulties for farmers. They constantly need to check on the state of their elevators, otherwise they are likely to encounter untold damage.

28

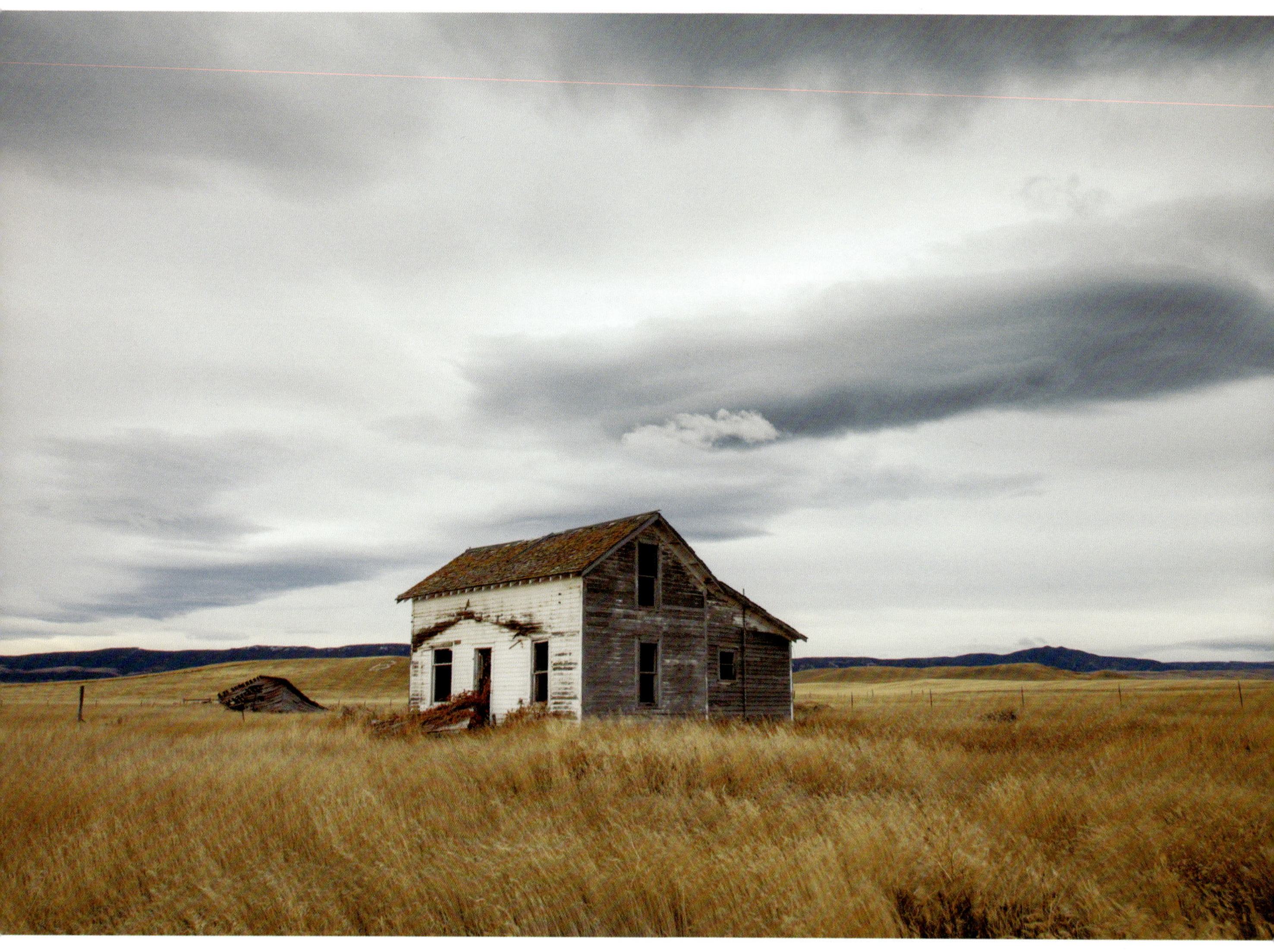

Deserted house, Judith Basin County

Extremes of weather, particularly the bitterly cold winds often blowing from Canada and the Arctic, could be one reason for the final abandonment of homes such as this.

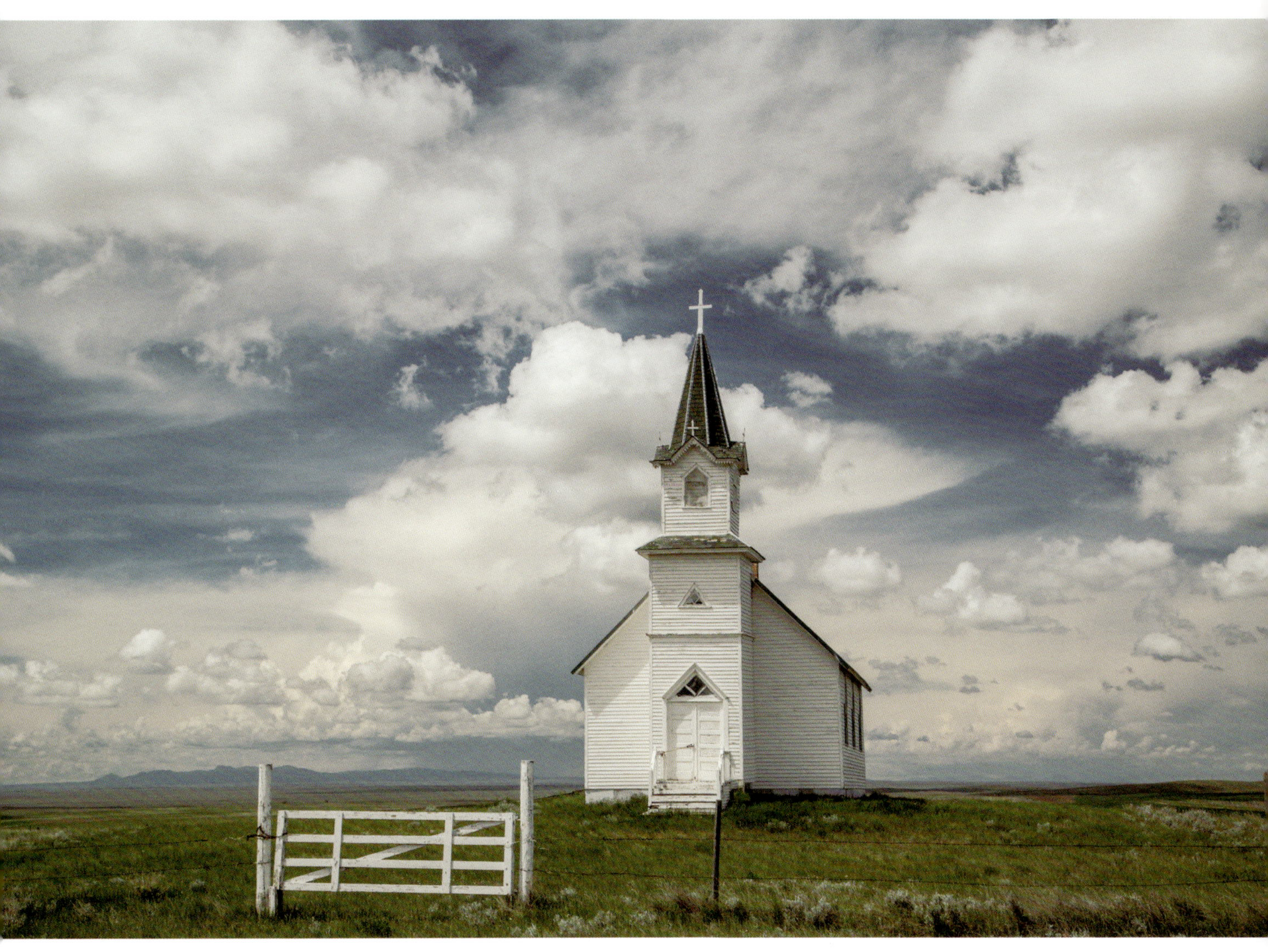

Scandia Lutheran Church, south of Malta

Accessed by driving along a dirt road, it is easy to wonder why a church was built in such a remote part of the county, but it was located to serve the spiritual needs of those living on outlying ranches and farms.

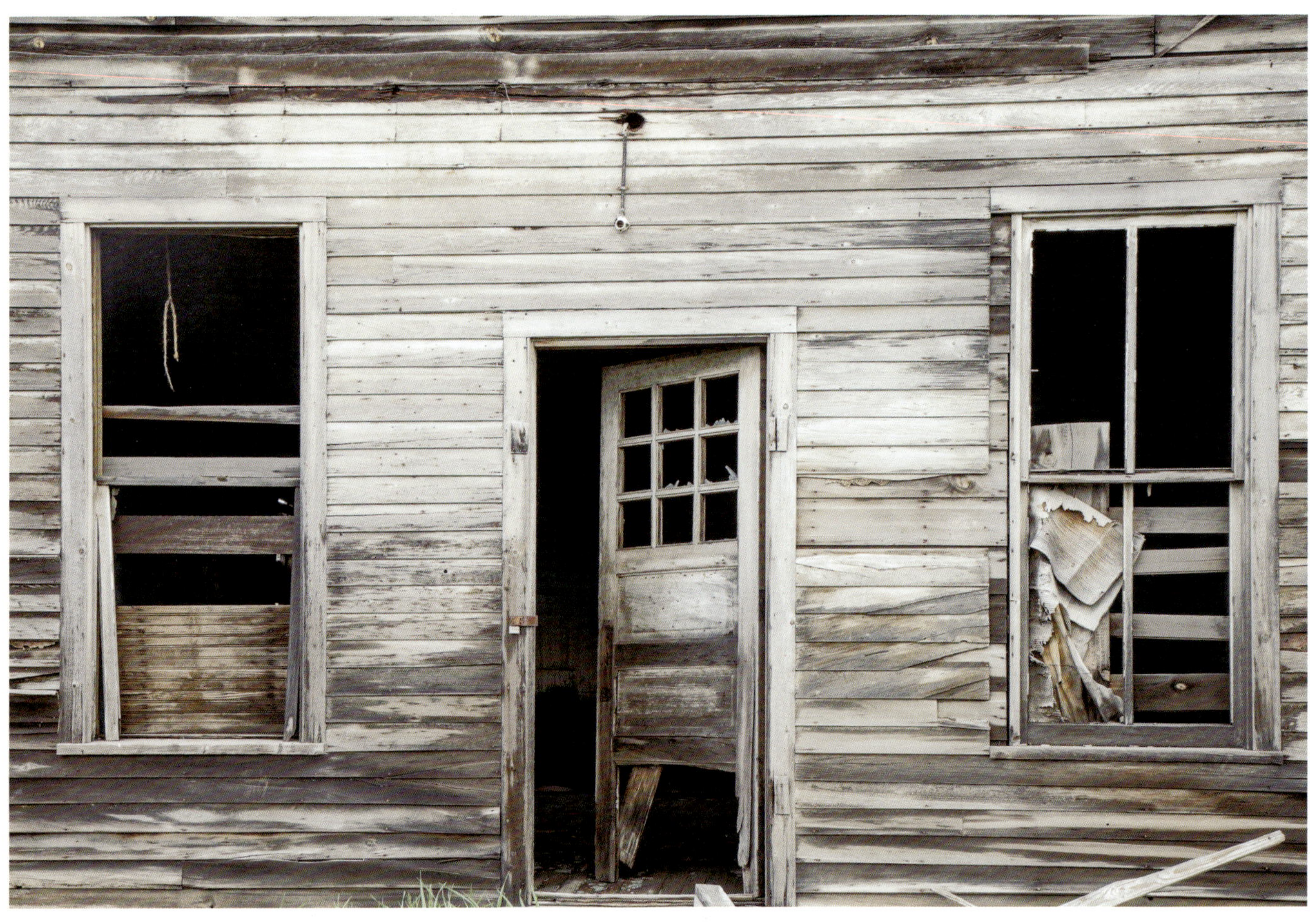

Façade, Musselshell County

Faded and weathered wooden facades often have an enigmatic quality about them. The open door is inviting, but it is always worth looking out for the occasional racoon, skunk or rattlesnake!

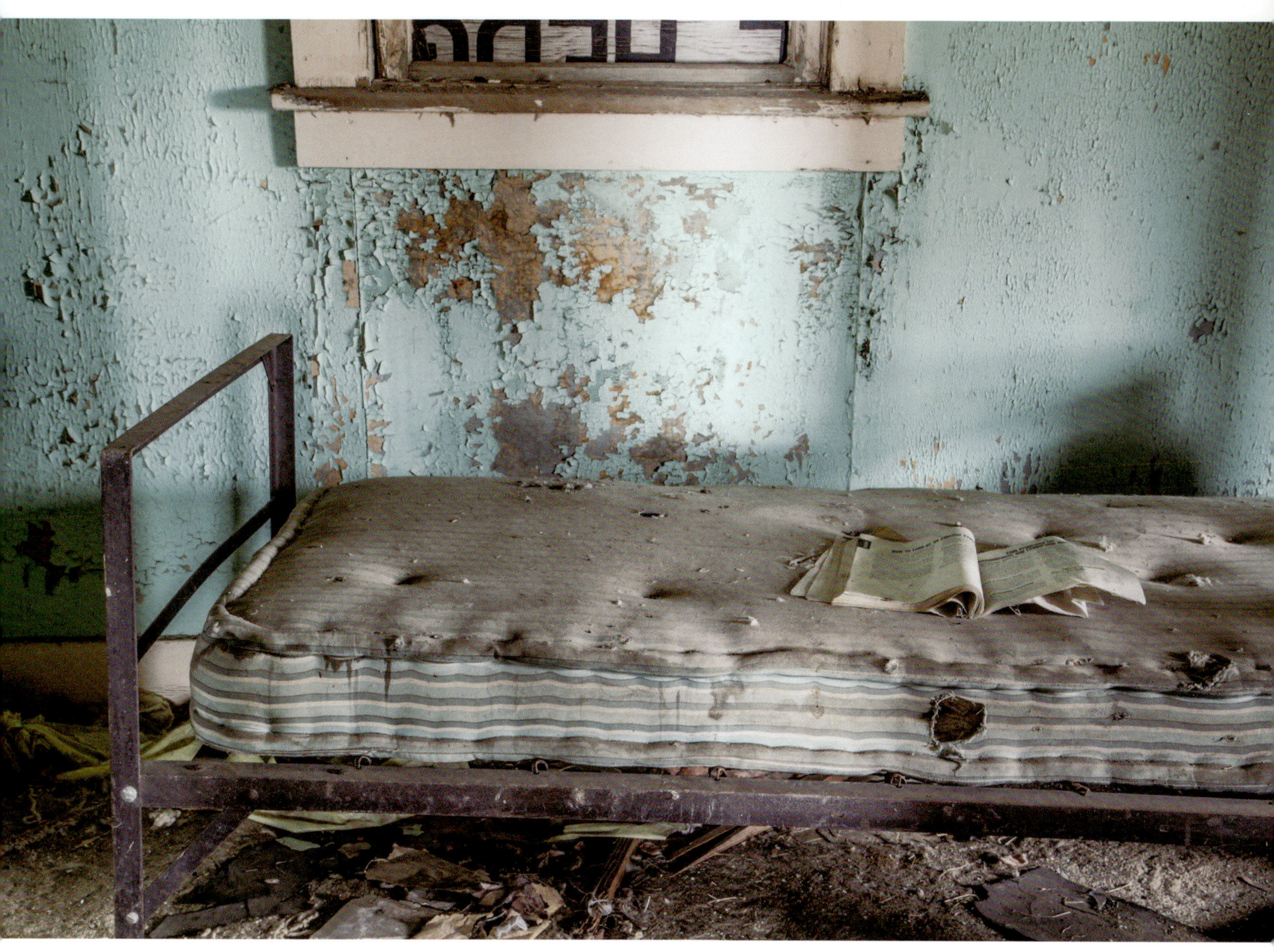

Interior with single bed, Ingomar

*Although this property was locked, I was able to take a shot through
a broken window. This sparsely furnished room gives an insight to
the harsh lives many who worked on the High Plains had to endure.*

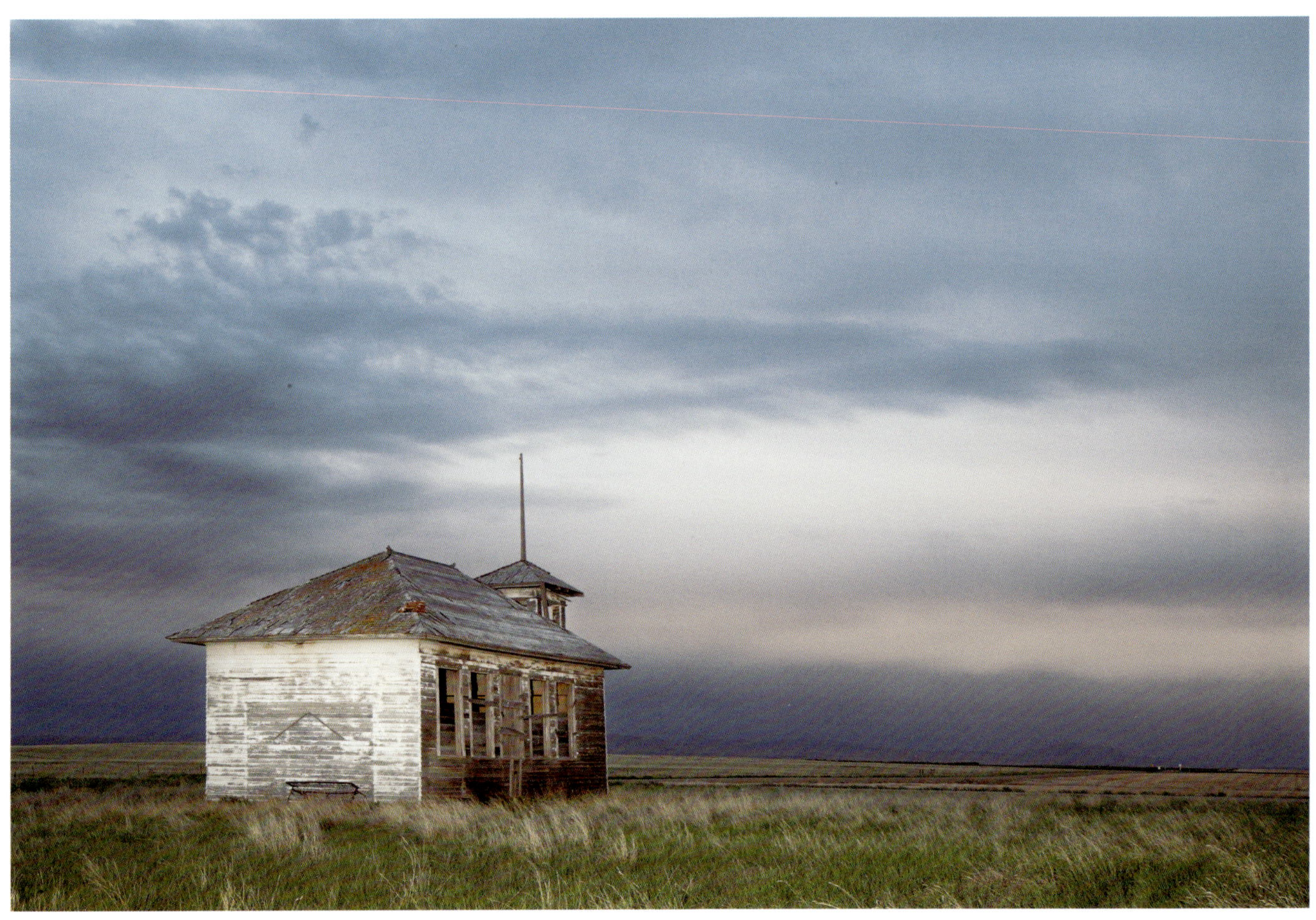

School at Burnham

Schools in the small rural communities were fairly functional, designed as single or double roomed constructions. Nevertheless, today they still make interesting subjects to photograph when viewed within the vastness of the High Plains. Located just off Highway 2, this fine old school serves as a welcome landmark as one travels west out of Havre.

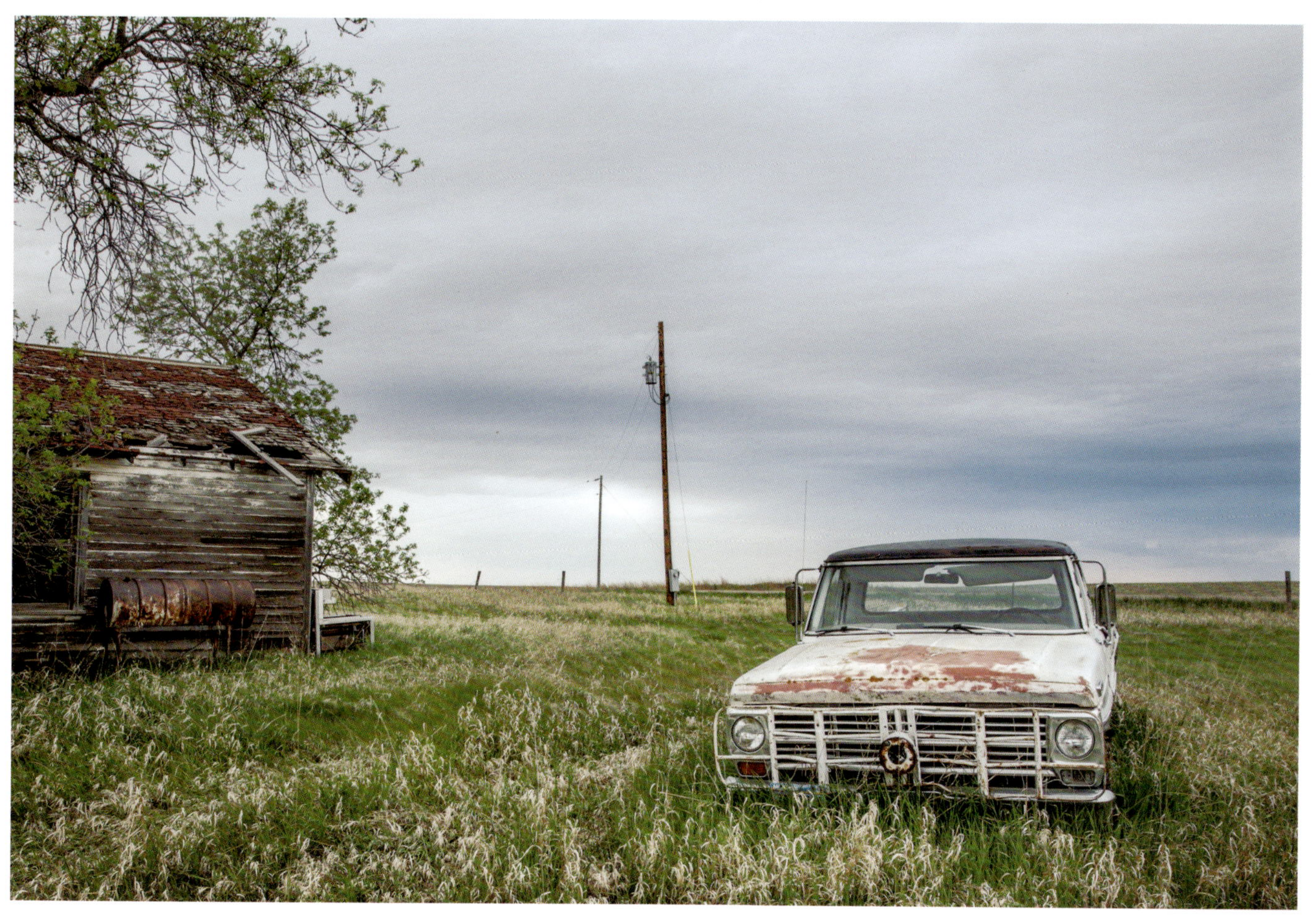

Deserted ranch, Sheridan County

*The abandoned vehicles which can often be seen at roadsides or on
deserted farms would often be used as a source for spare parts.*

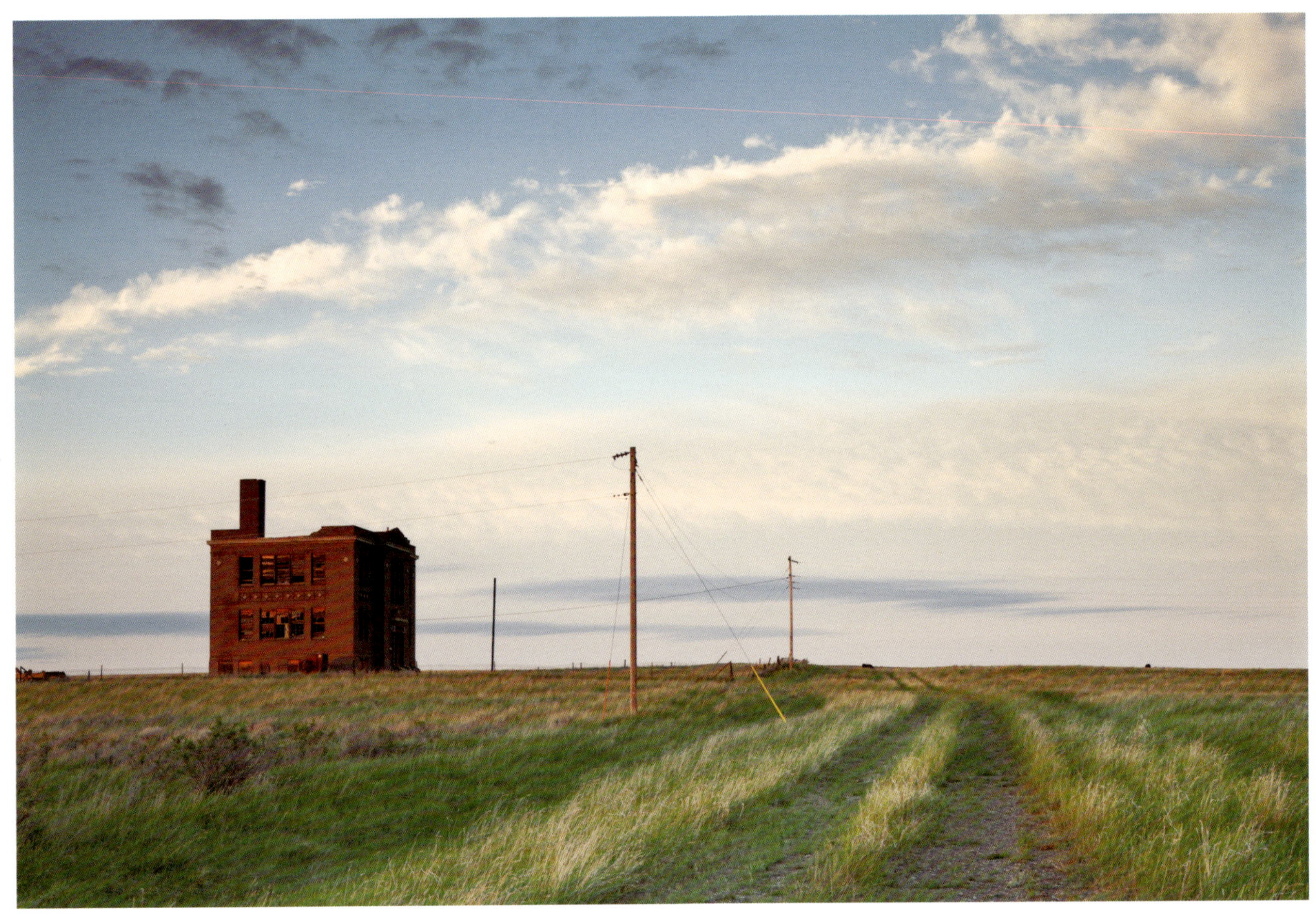

Vananda school

After homesteaders were attracted to this arid part of Montana by the disingenuous promises of the railroad company, the school was established round about 1925. The population quickly depleted because of the difficulties of farming in such an area.

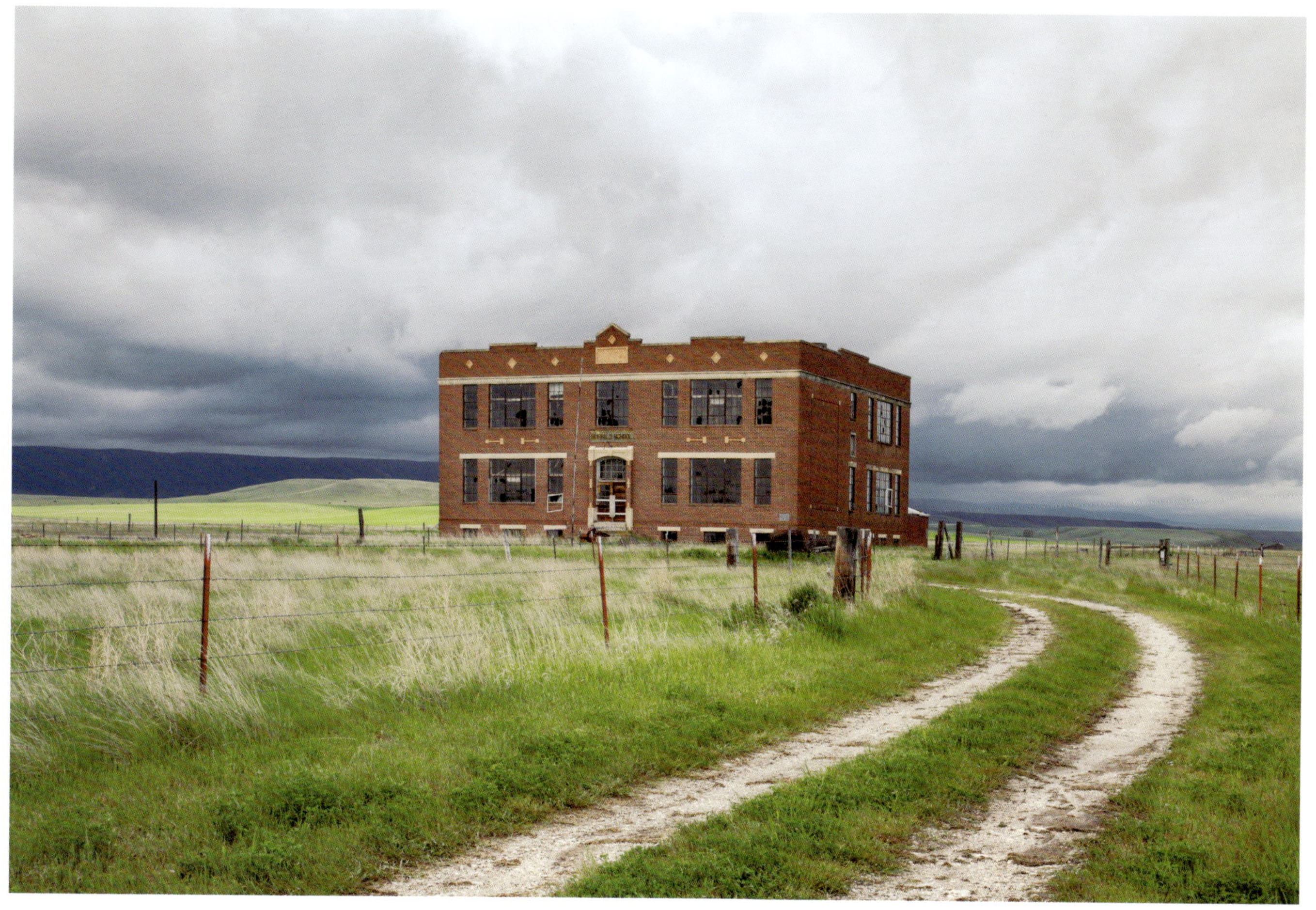

Old red brick school

*After building a modest home, the first priority of the early settlers
was to construct a school, showing the value placed on education.
The size of this iconic old building gives some idea of the original
population of the community, which now numbers less than 100
for the whole postal area.*

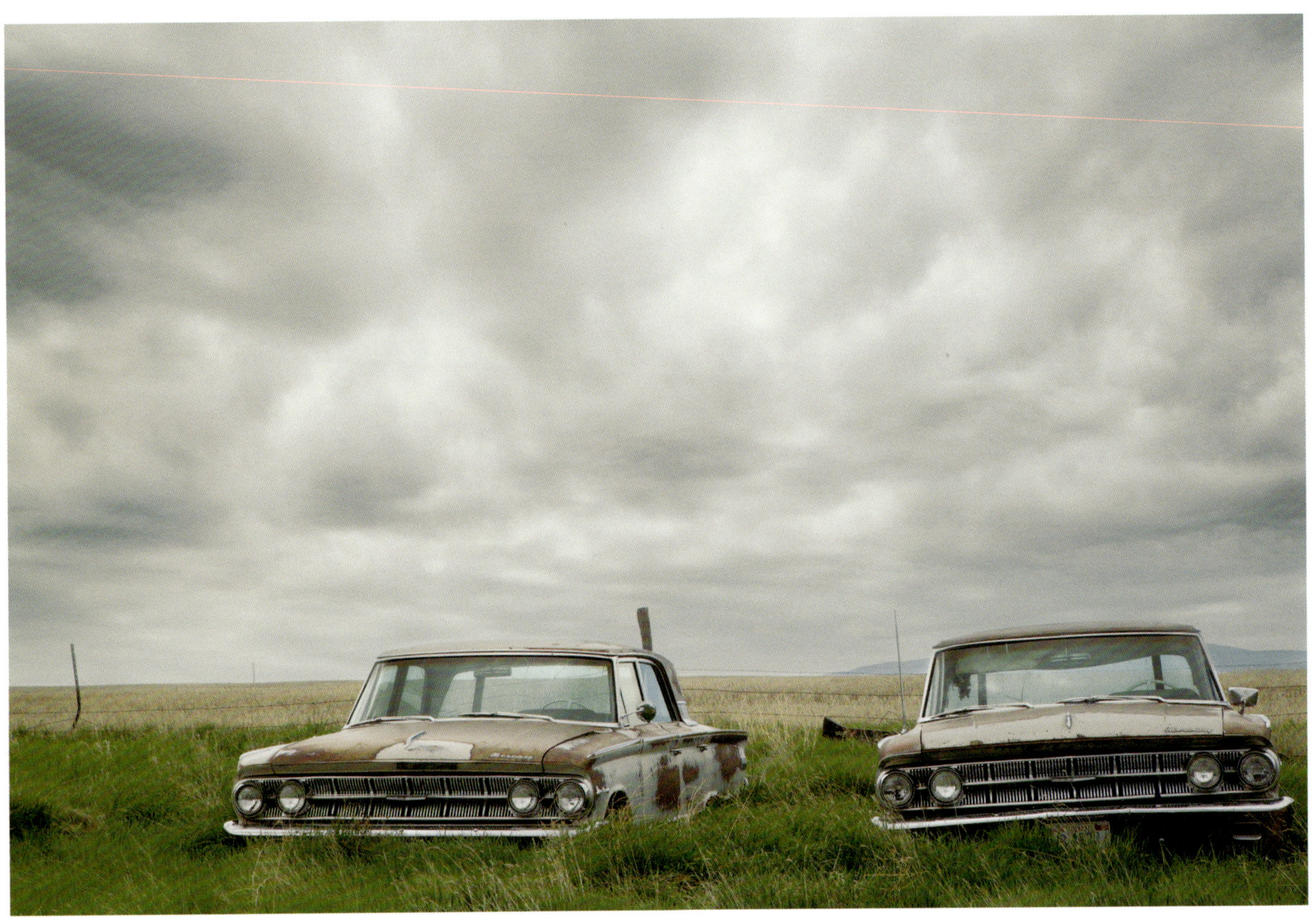

Two abandoned Mercurys

It is easy to imagine that discarded vehicles such as these have some scrap-value, but with such a depleted local population, they remain absolutely worthless.

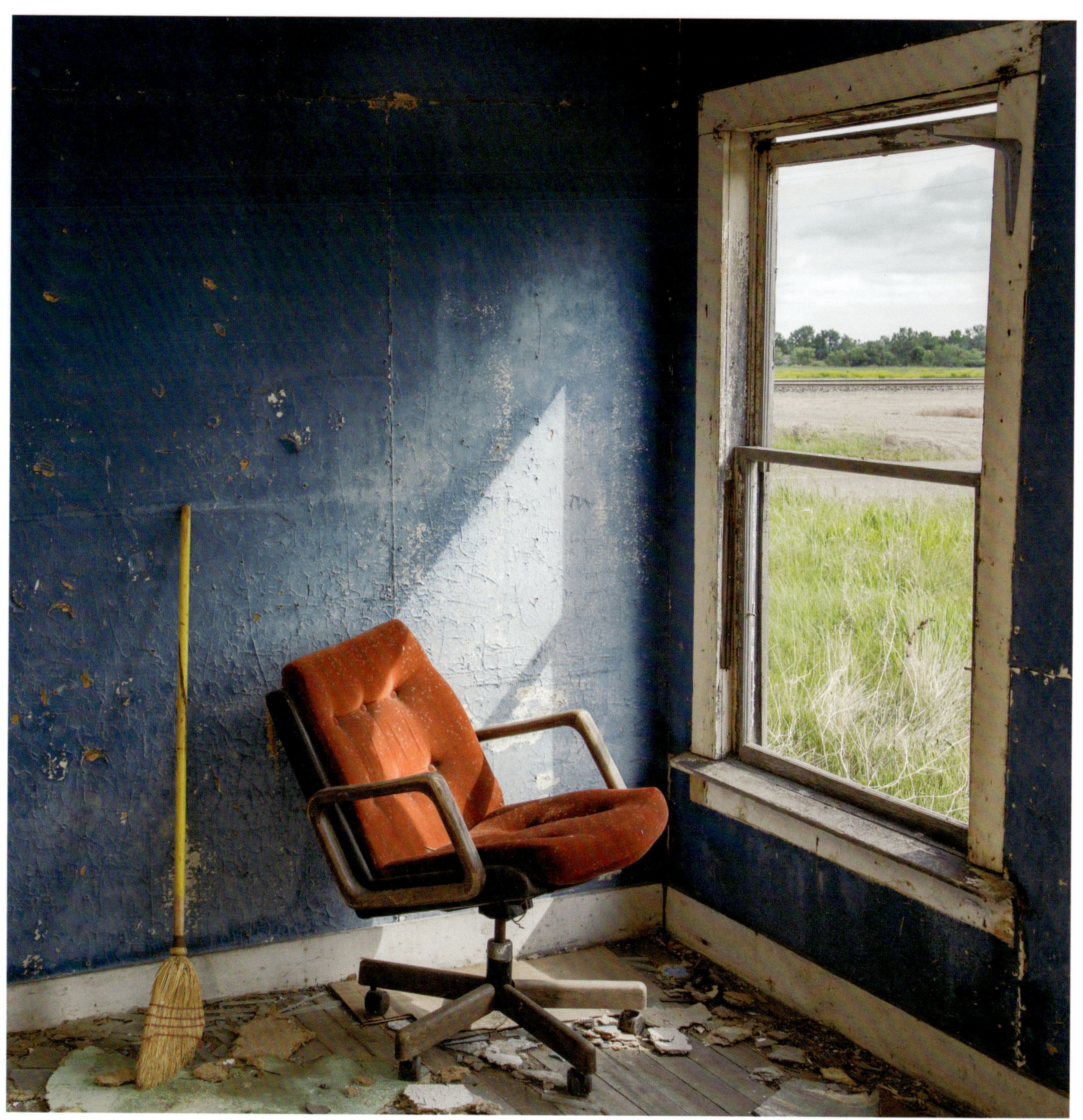

Interior with red chair, Hathaway

Prior to the construction of Interstate 94, much of the traffic would pass through Hathaway; now the entire community has been abandoned.

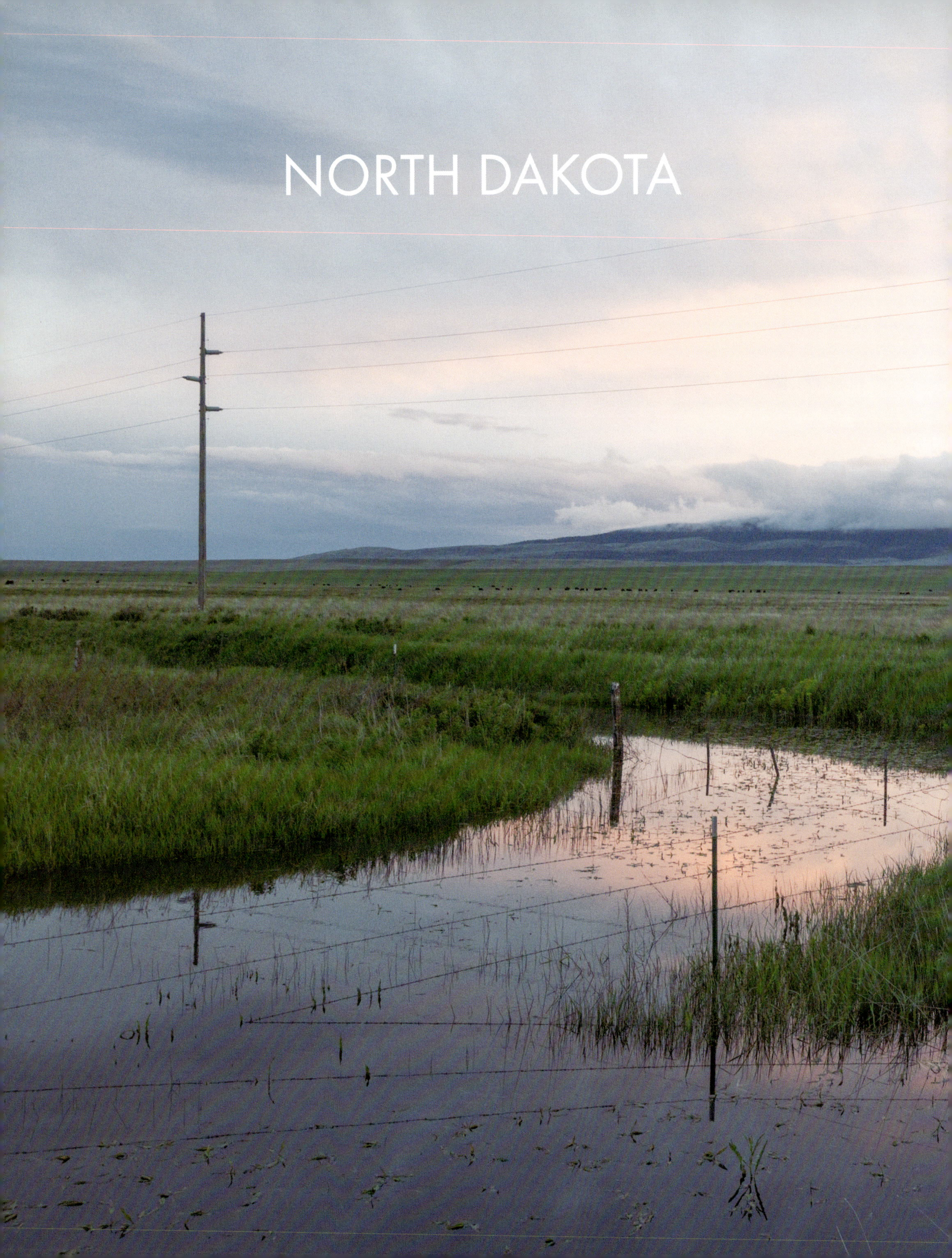
NORTH DAKOTA

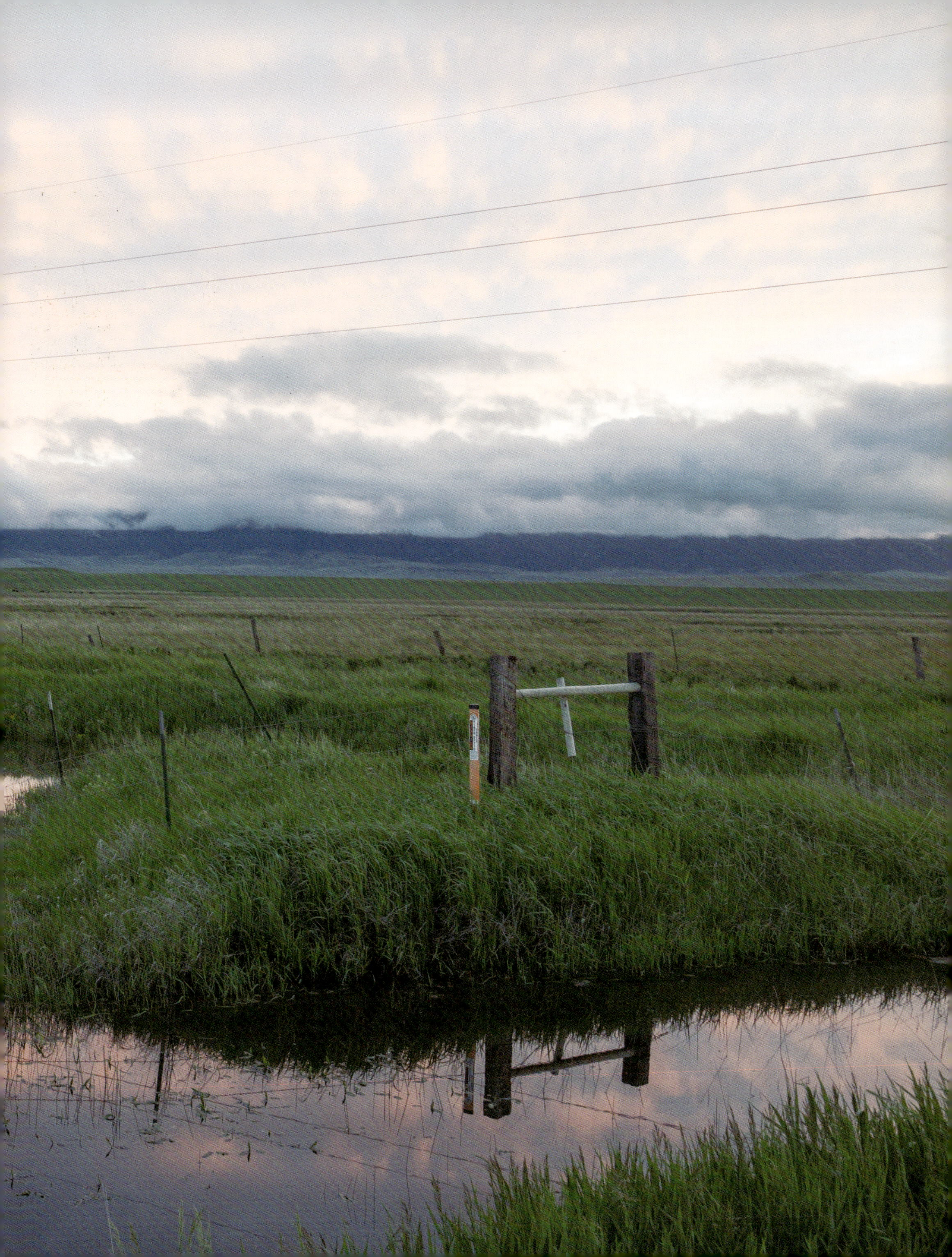

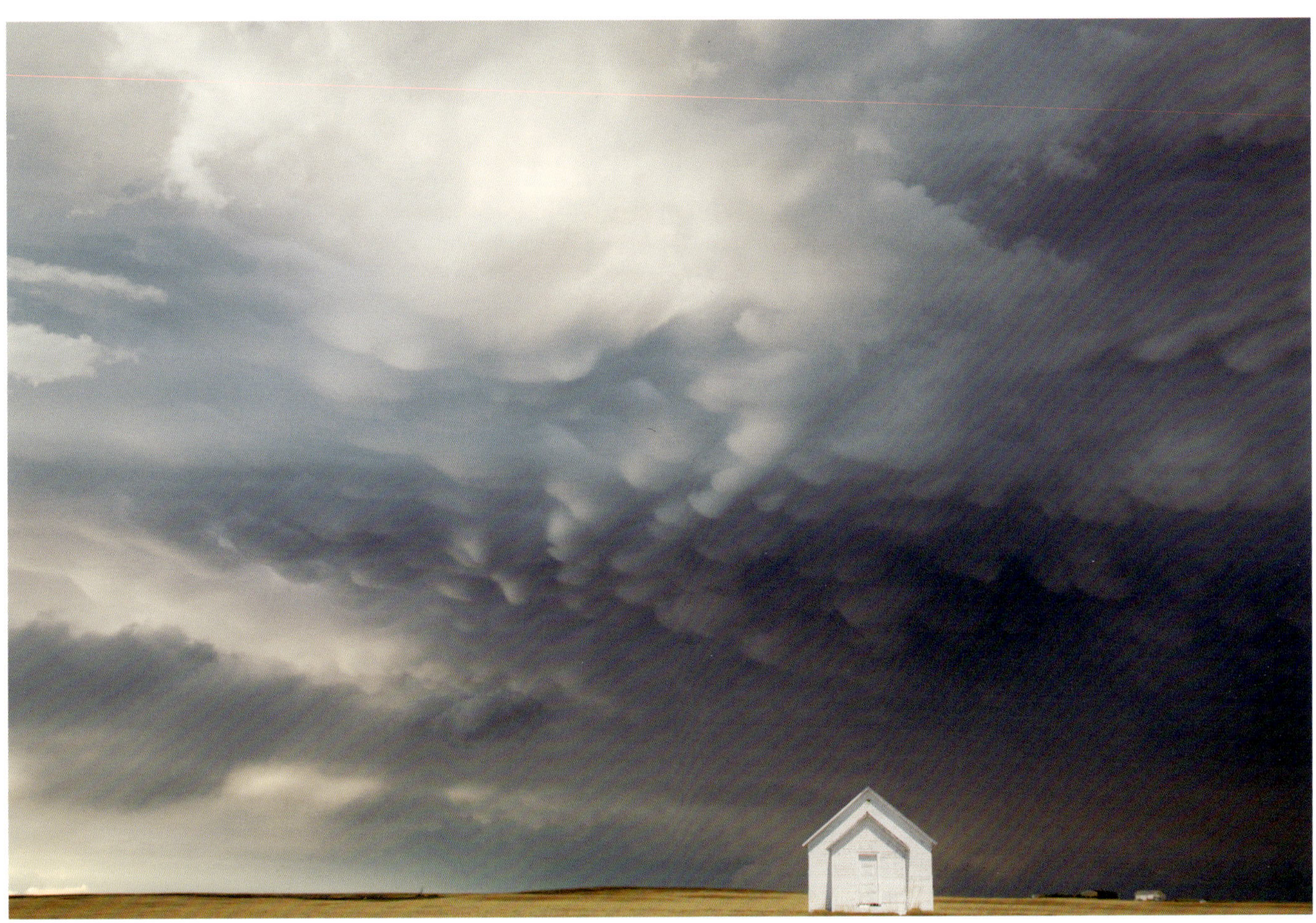

Small white school, near Robinson

We had been experiencing very heavy storms which produced astonishing skies. Isolated on the wide prairie, this building appears dwarfed by the menacing clouds.

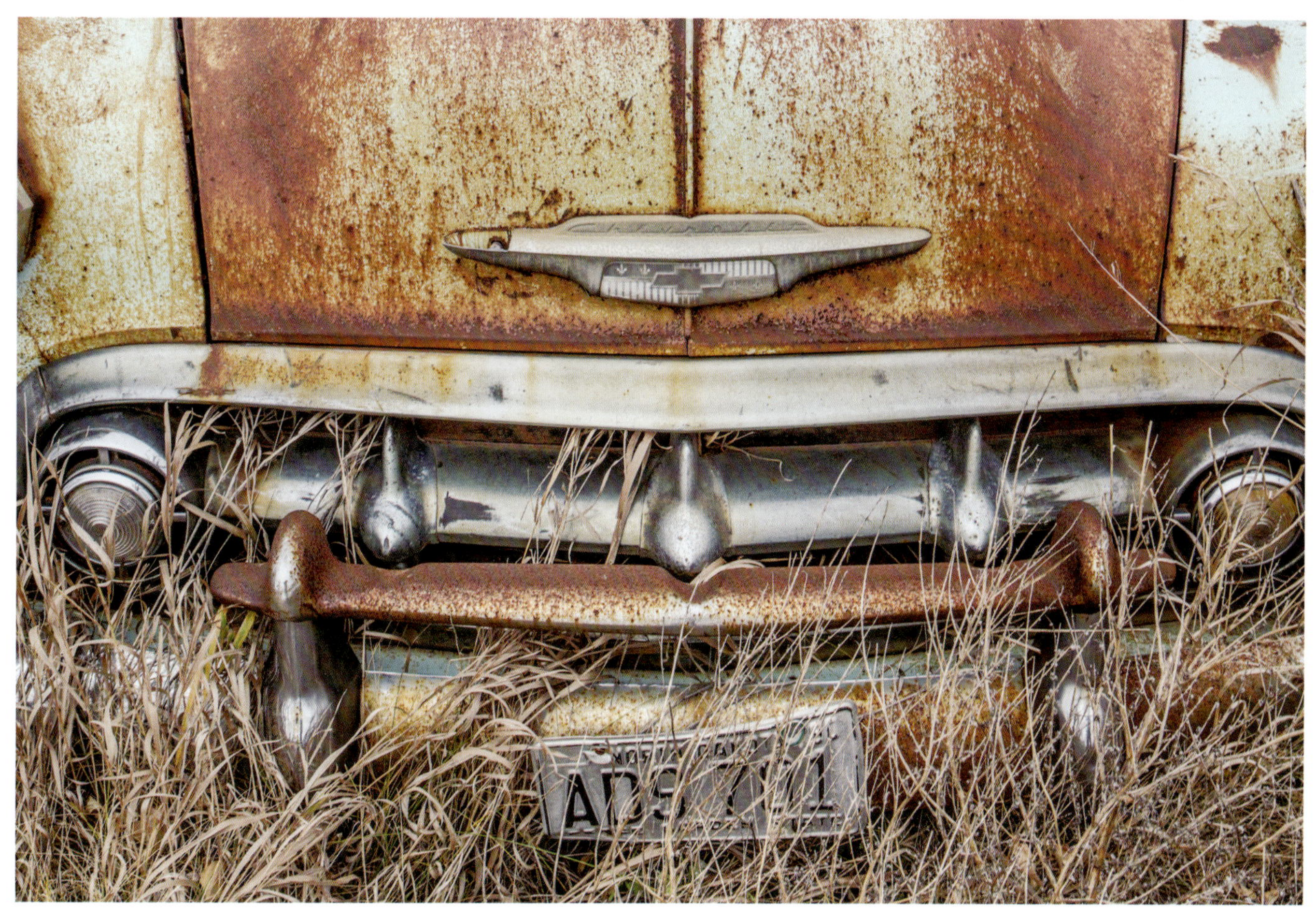

▲

Rusting Chevvy

*While we often aimed to photograph these wonderful old vehicles
within the landscape in which they lay, occasionally we were
attracted to the rich detail.*

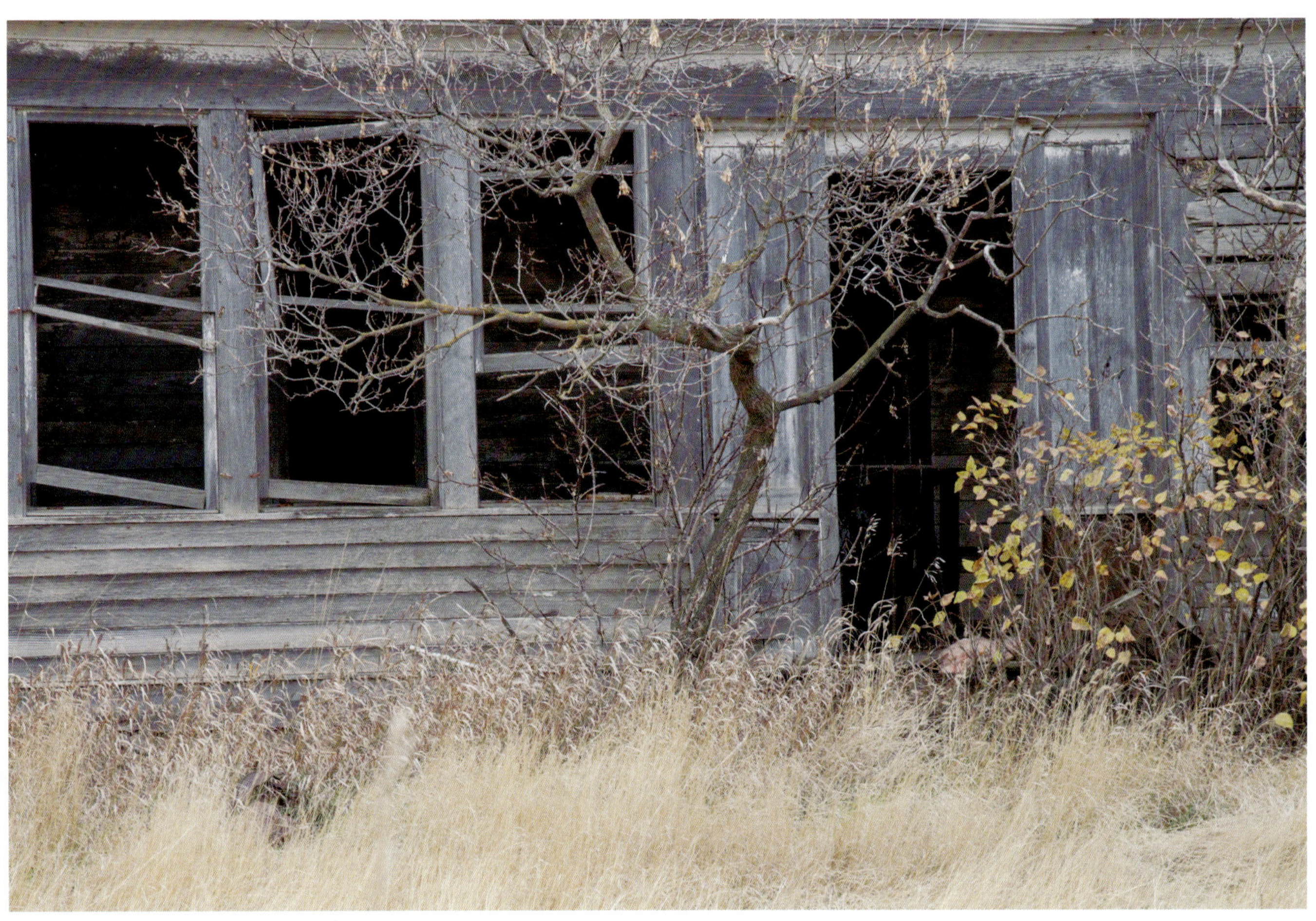

Crumbling facade, Divide County

*There eventually comes a time when the earth appears to be
trying to reclaim these deteriorating buildings.*

Lone house near Hwy2

*Unless houses were regularly painted they would soon fall into disrepair
due to the searing summer heat and harsh winters on the plains.*

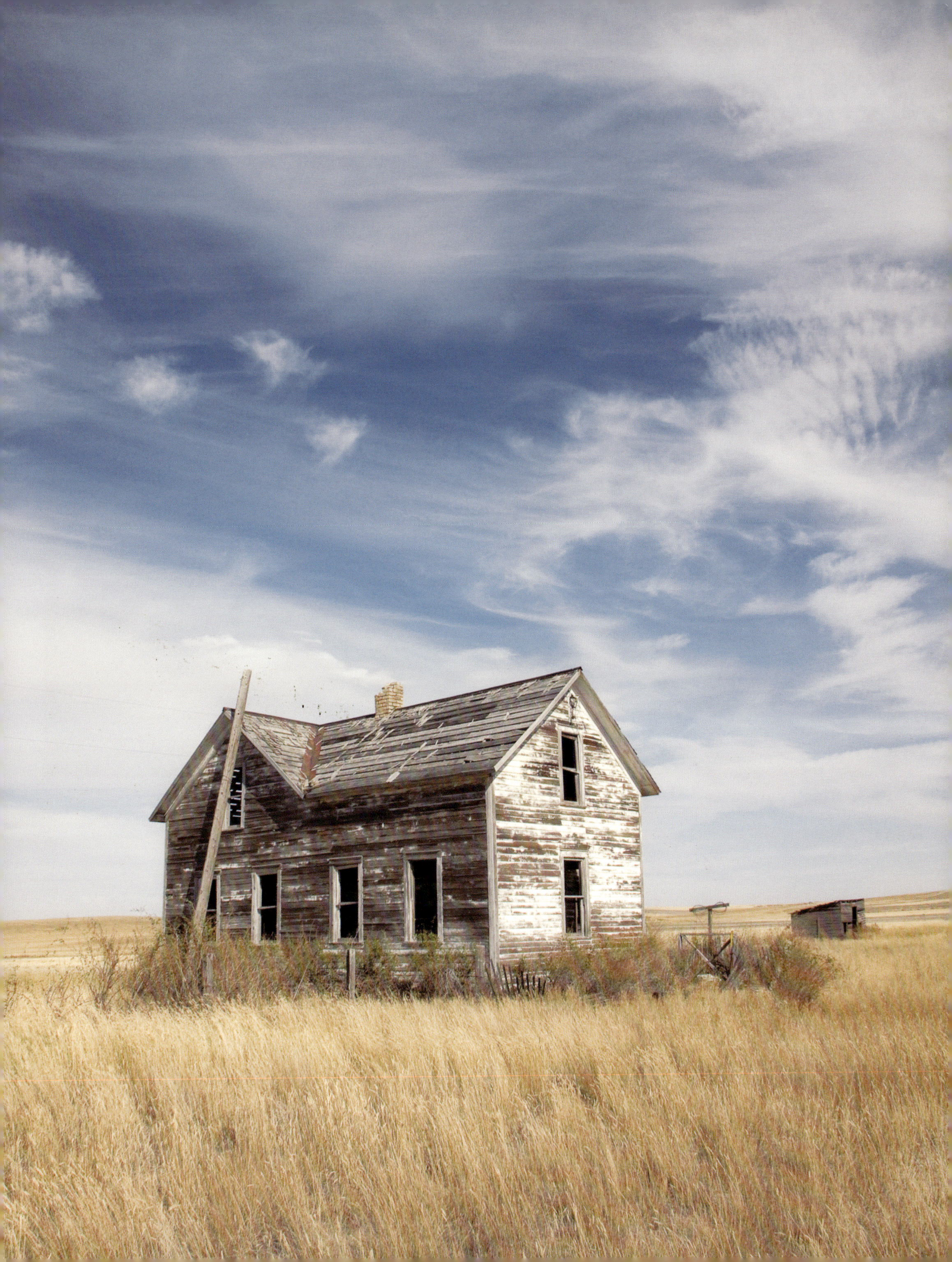

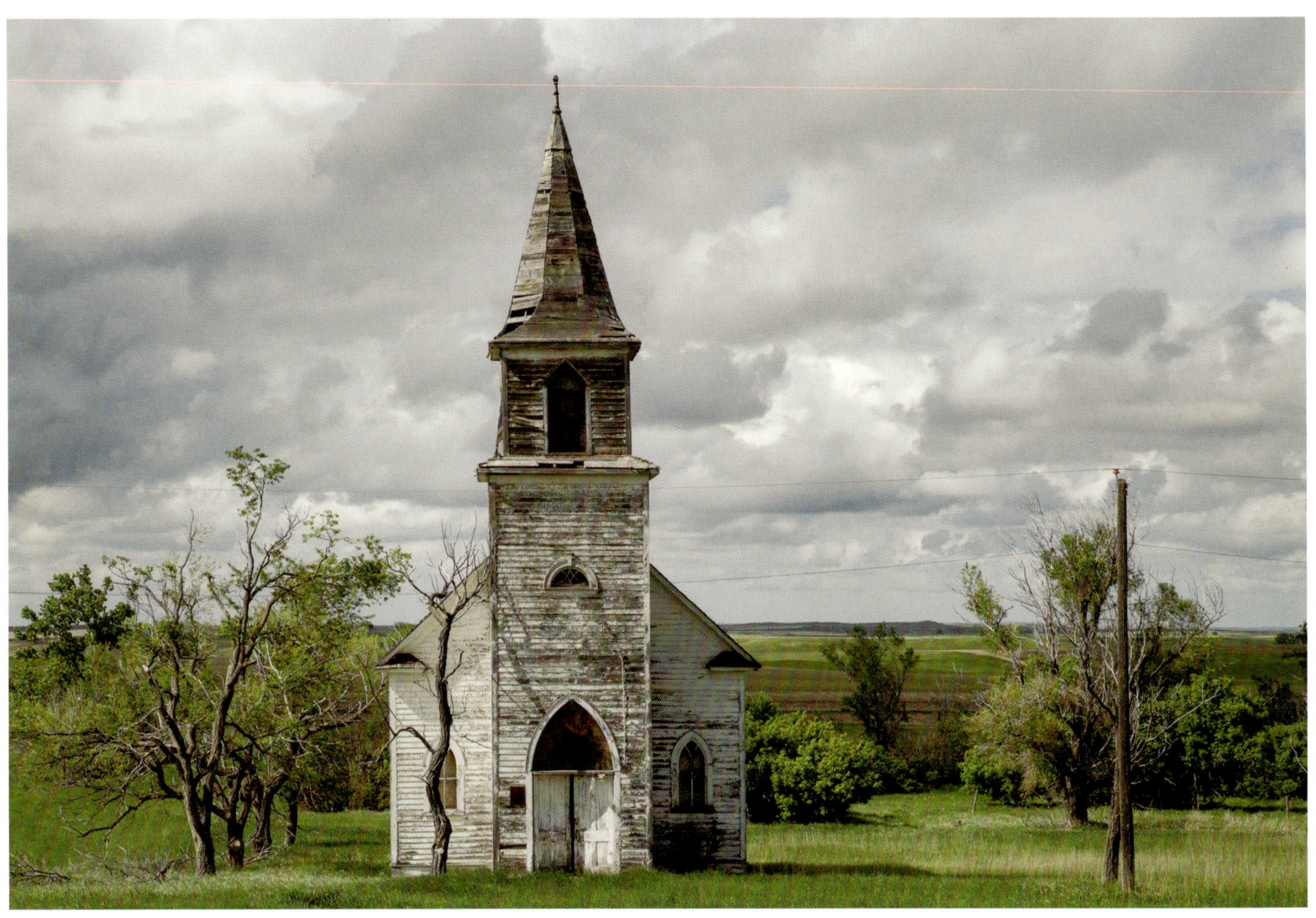

▲

Church at Heil

Church-going is an important part of the lives of many of the communities on the High Plains, so to see a building in such a state of disrepair is a measure of how much the town has declined in recent years.

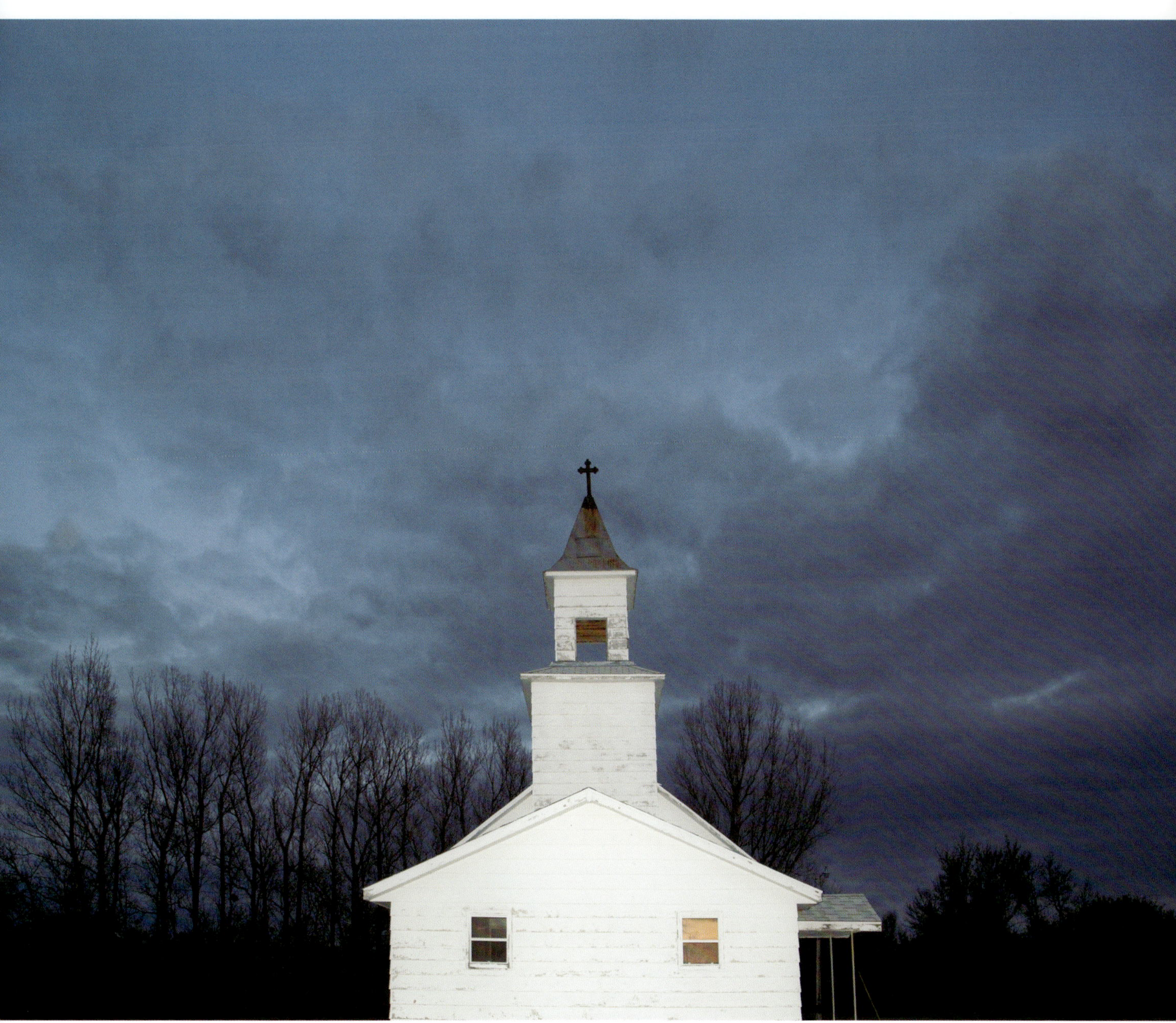

Church at Linton

It is often the design of the churches, based on vernacular Scandinavian architecture, which proves to be so appealing. Constructed of timber and painted white, they are visible for miles. Photographed in late evening light, flash was used to illuminate the gable-end of this fine old building.

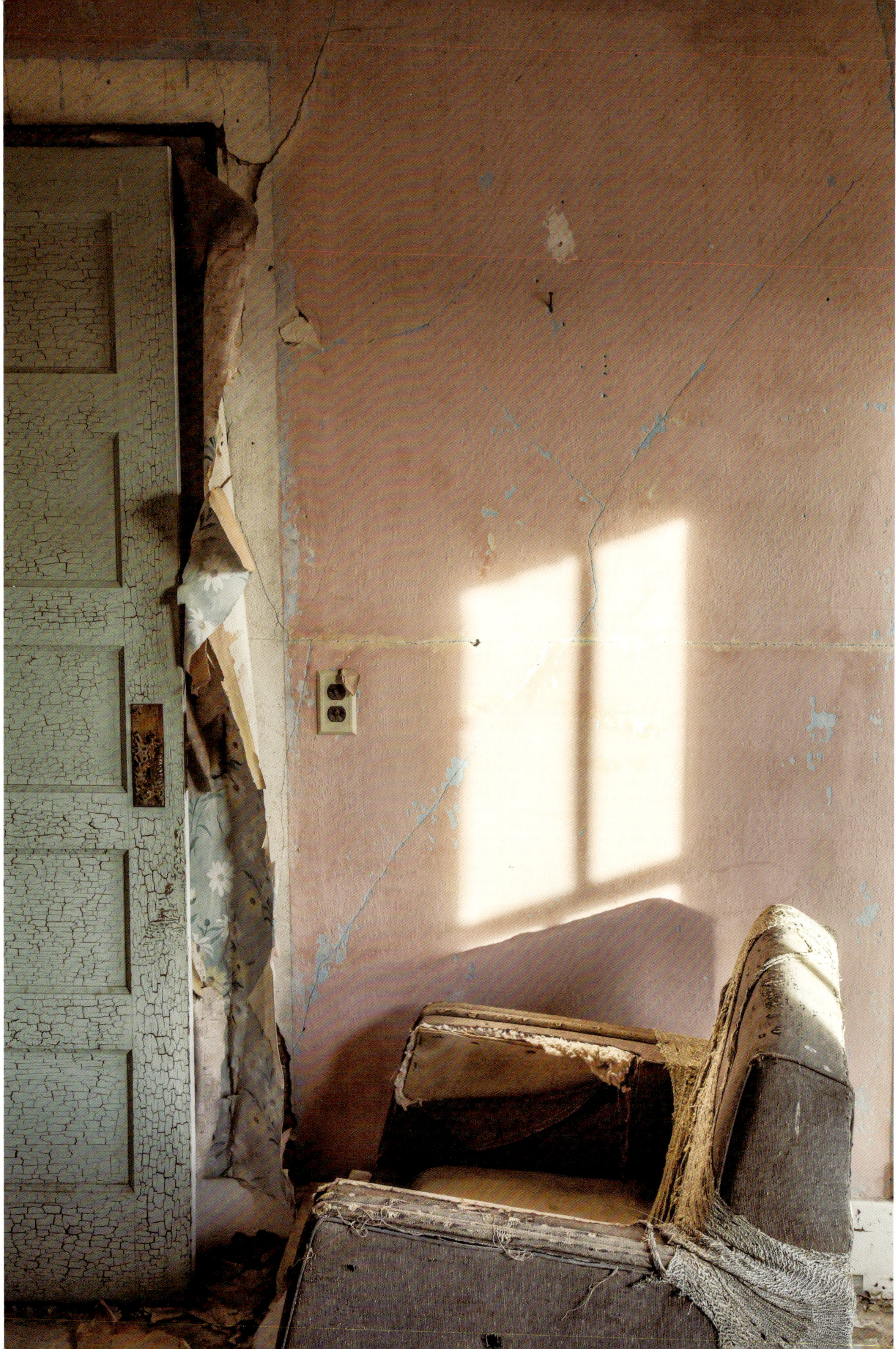

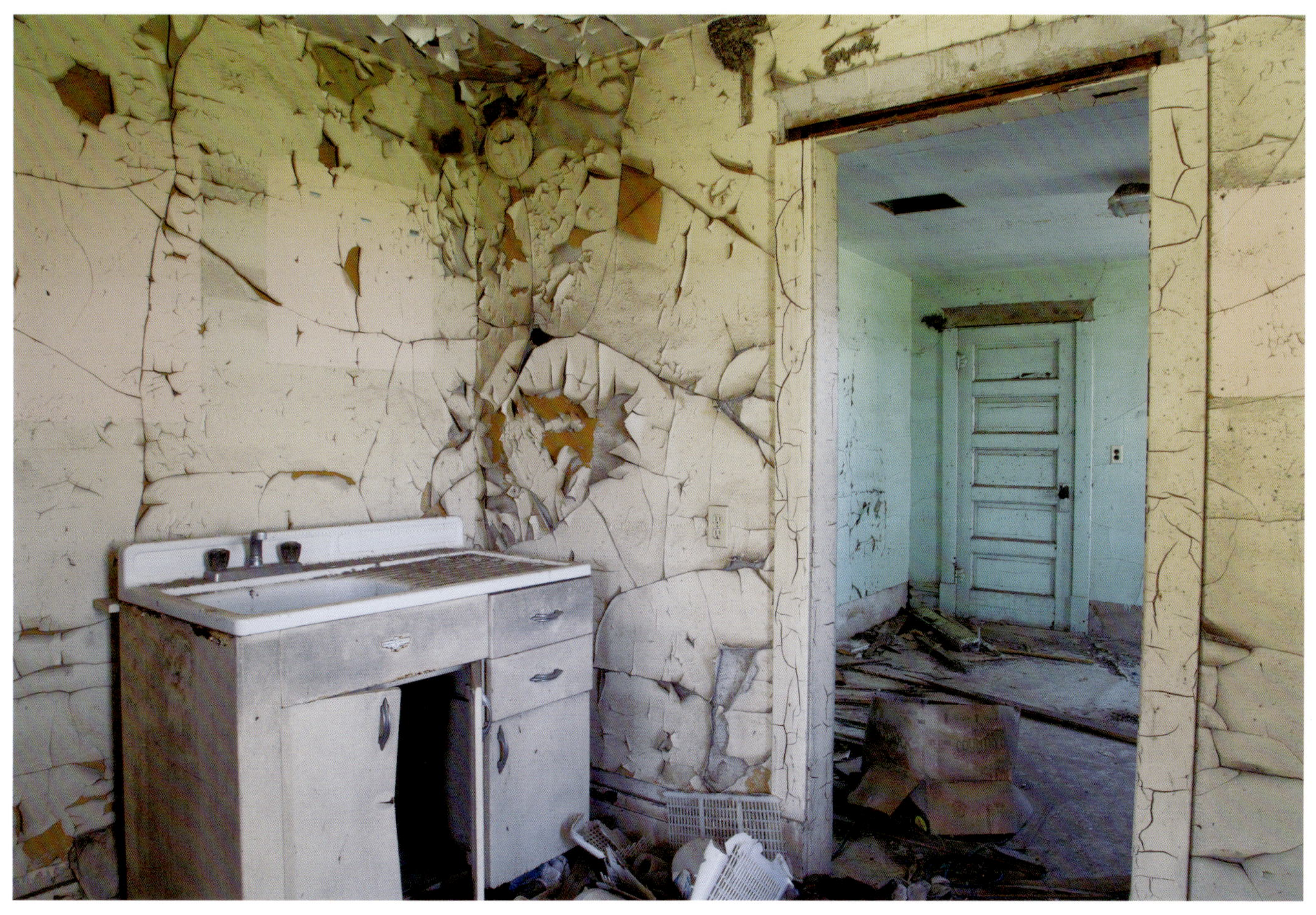

Interior with kitchen sink and green door,
abandoned house, Manfred

*While many of the properties we entered were stripped, much of
the "white furniture" remains. As these properties gradually decayed,
it is quite illuminating to see how well this kitchen sink fared.*

Chair and green door

*When entering a building that was once someone's home, it is so
tempting to imagine those that once lived there and speculate on
their tastes and preferences.*

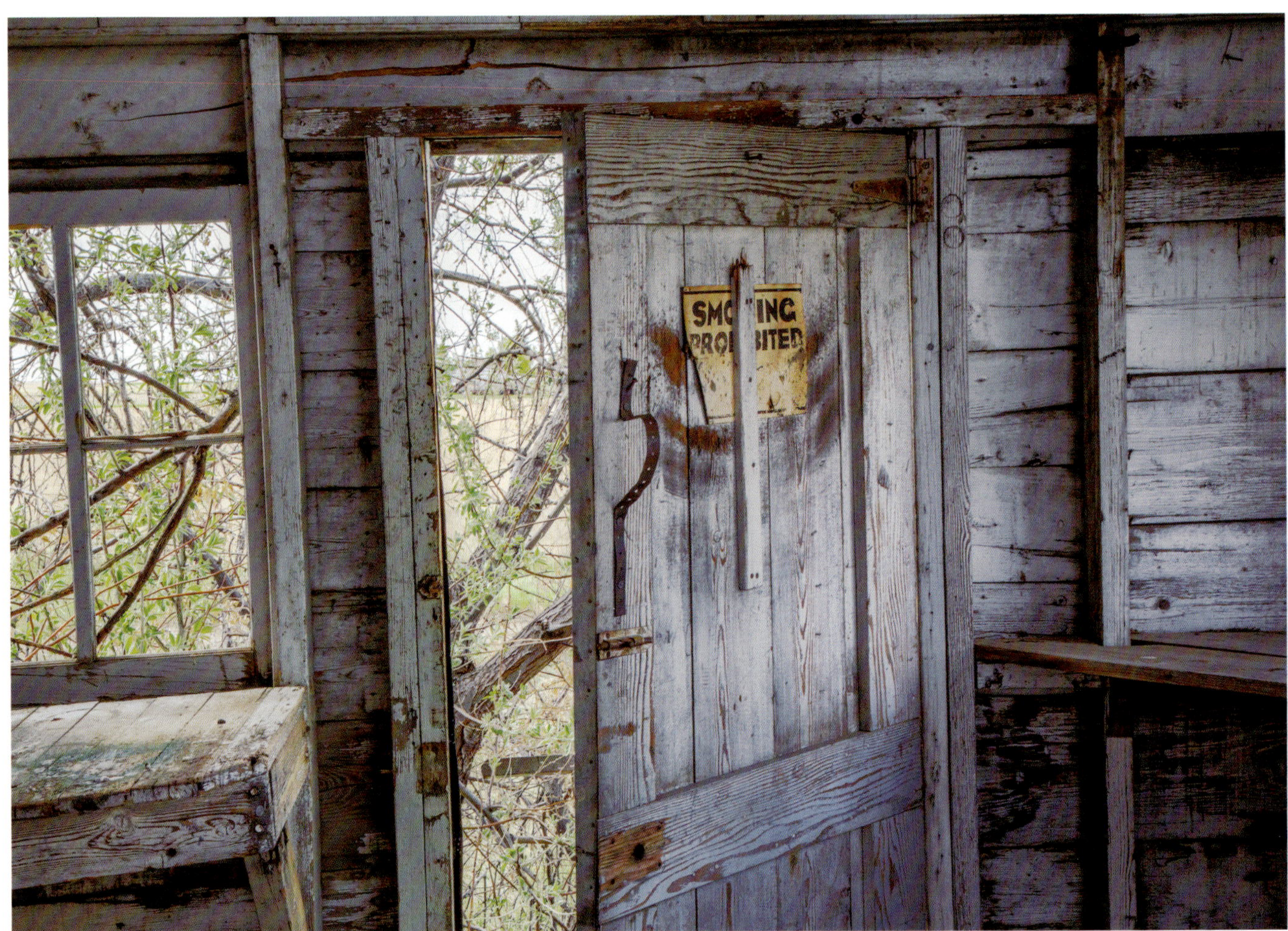

Smoking Prohibited: interior of elevator

When entering an abandoned elevator, one sometimes needs a reminder that this was once a workplace for dozens of men and women.With enormous stores of grain, the threat of fire was a constant hazard.

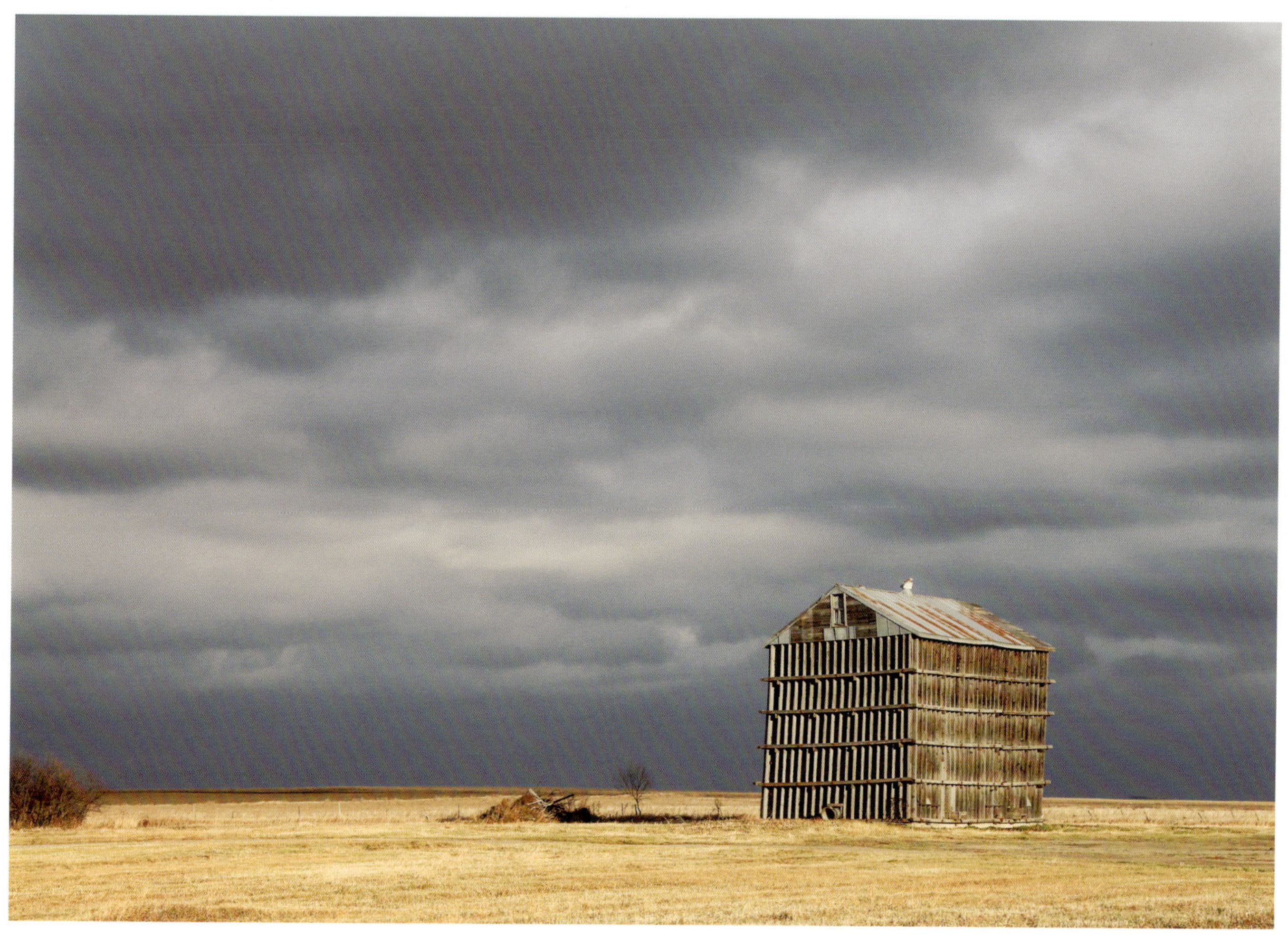

Old barn, Zeeland

*Not surprisingly, Zeeland was named by the Dutch immigrants
who settled here near the border with South Dakota in 1902.*

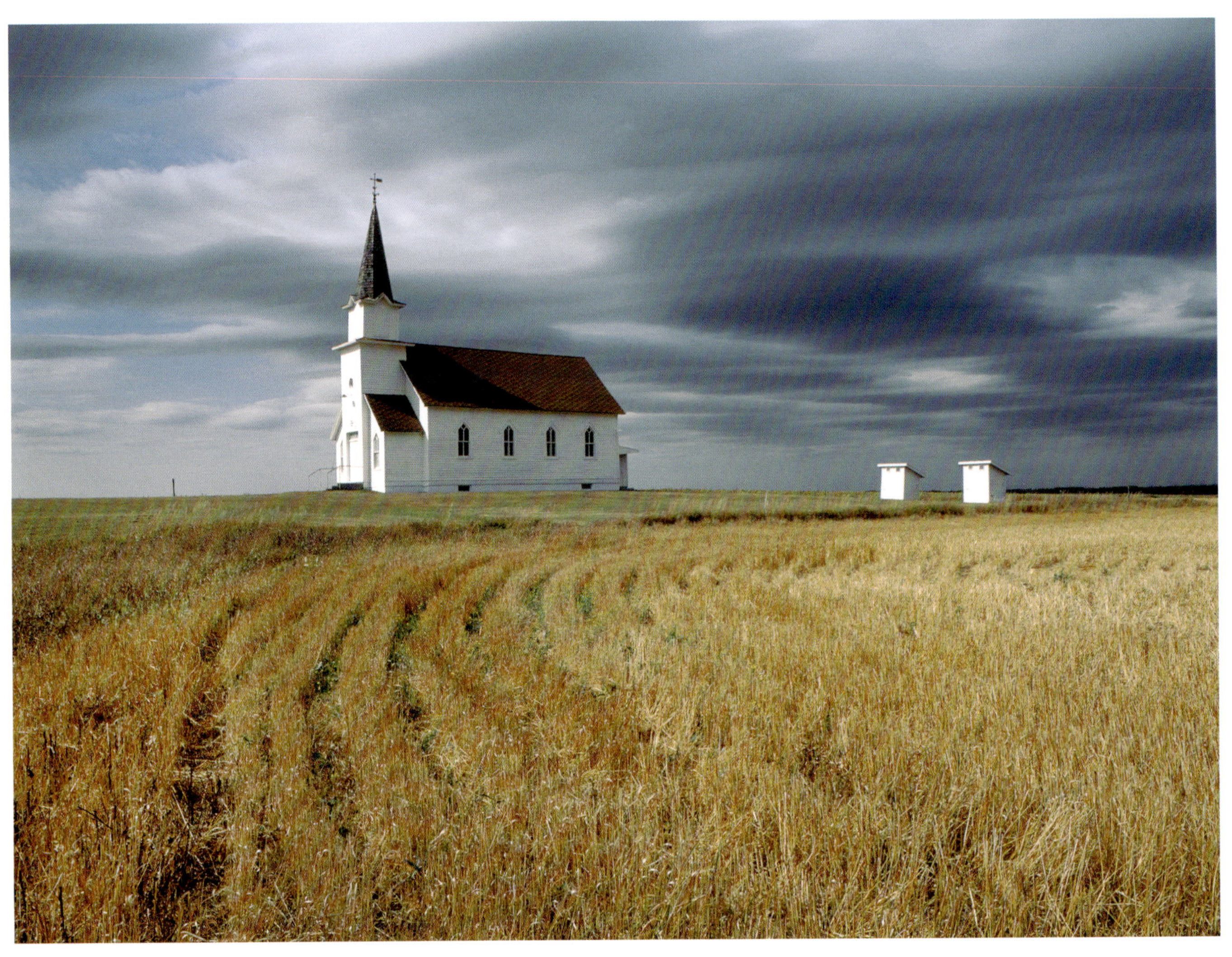

Kassel Reformed Church, Sheridan County

This iconic old church set high on the prairie west of Hwy 14 can be seen for miles around and would have been accessible for the surrounding farms and small communities. The two small white structures were the toilets!

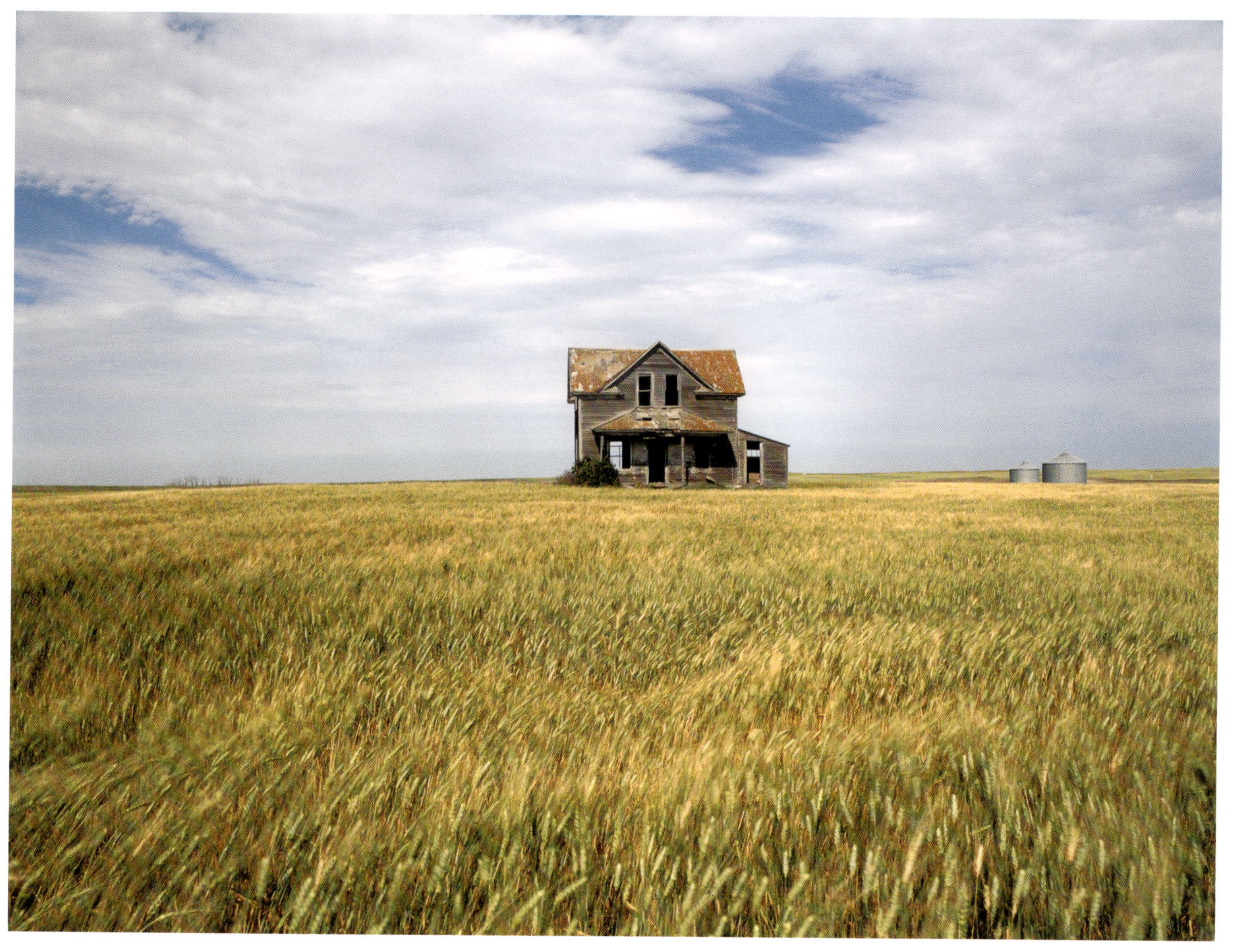

House in wheat field near Corinth

One of our favourite buildings over the years, this once fine house today stands amid construction work linked to the fracking boom and is probably destined for destruction.

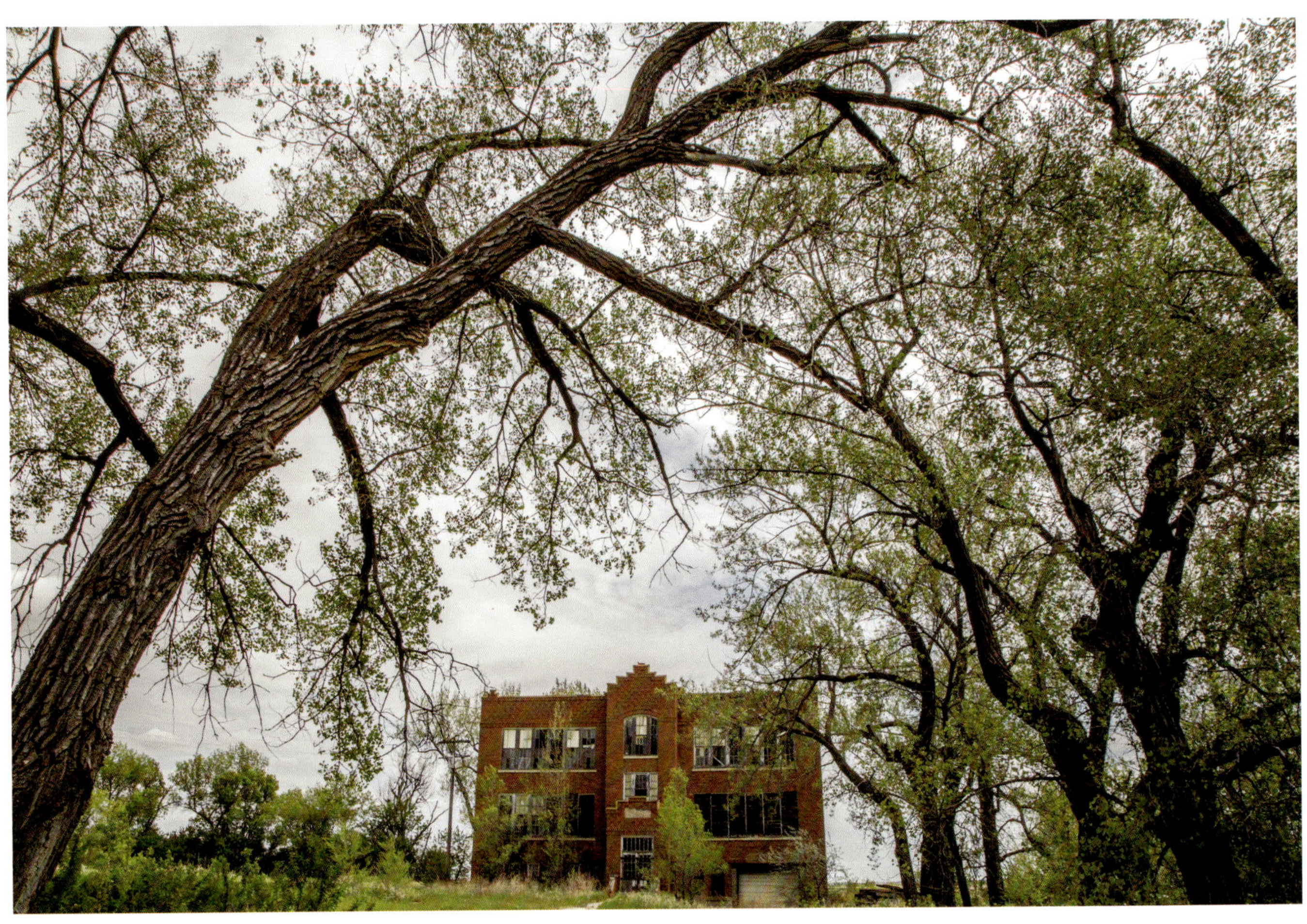

Old School

*When coming across a substantially built brick school such as
this, we are reminded that it once served a community of more
than 400 children. It now serves as a sad icon of the extent of the
depopulation this area has suffered.*

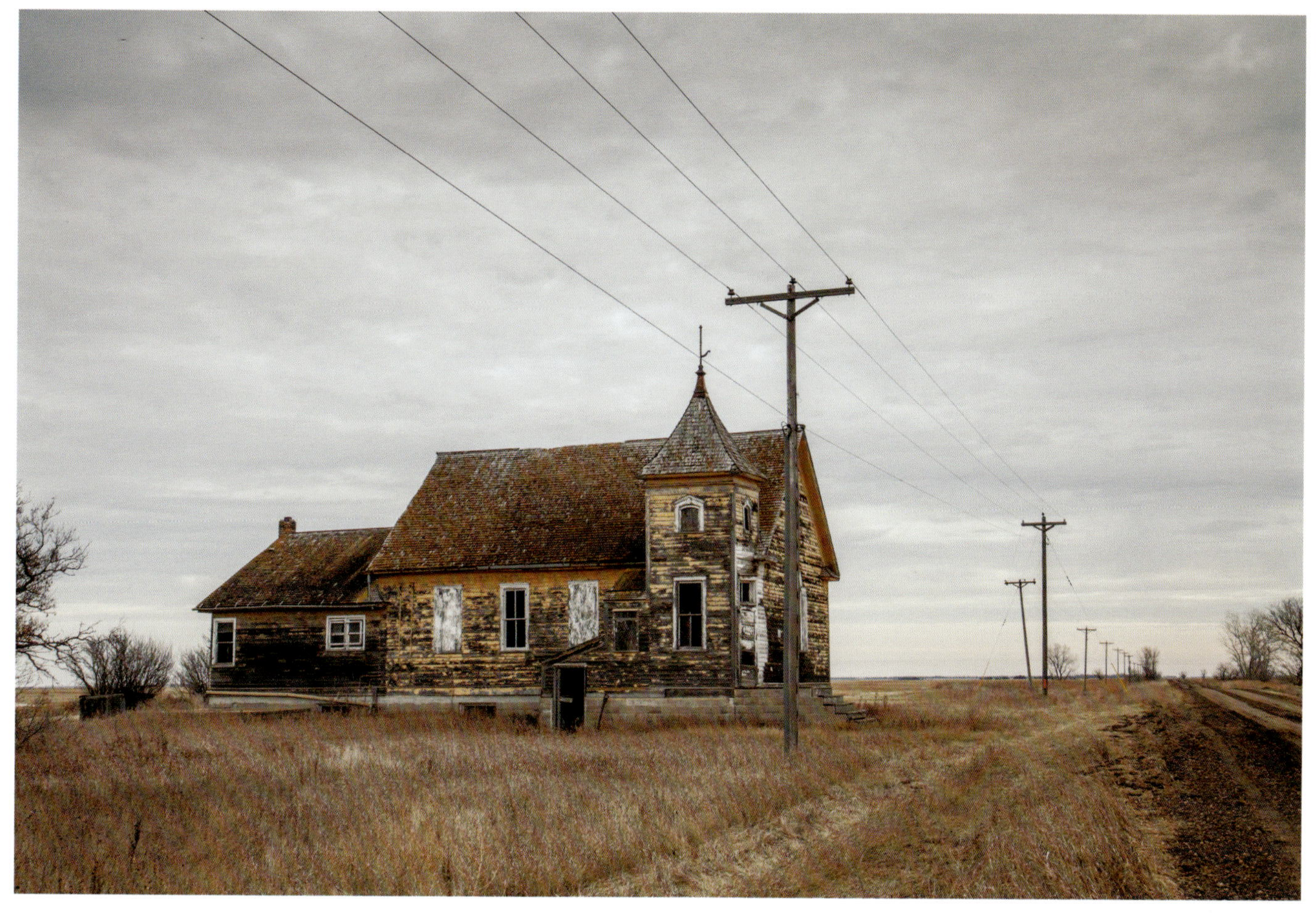

Church west of Minot

Ten years ago it was incredibly rare to come across a seemingly abandoned church, but now this is becoming a more frequent occurrence, reflecting the continuing drop in the local churchgoing population.

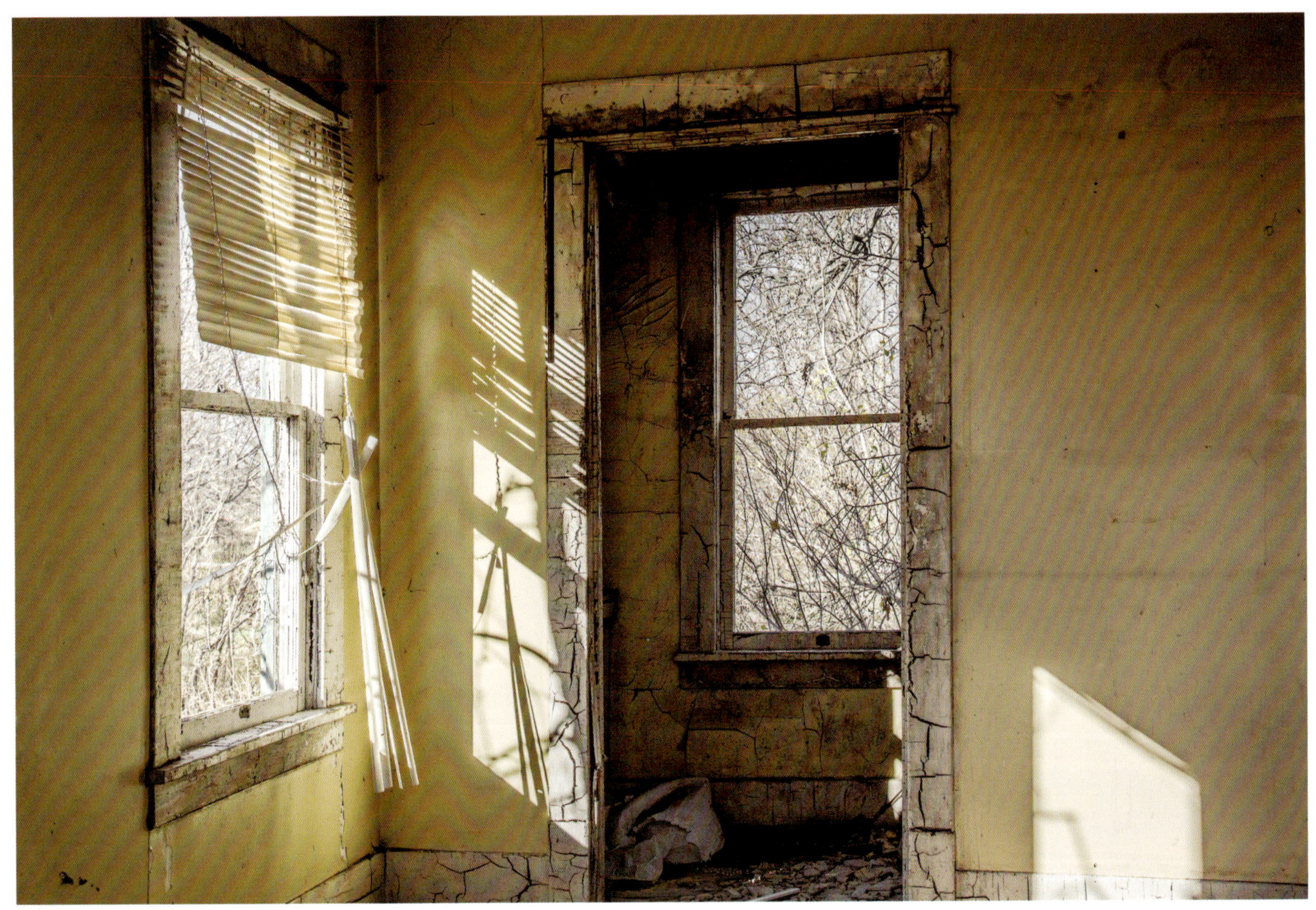

▲

Yellow interior

*Devoid of furniture, this interior nevertheless offers great interest as
the outside light created interesting patterns on the bare walls.*

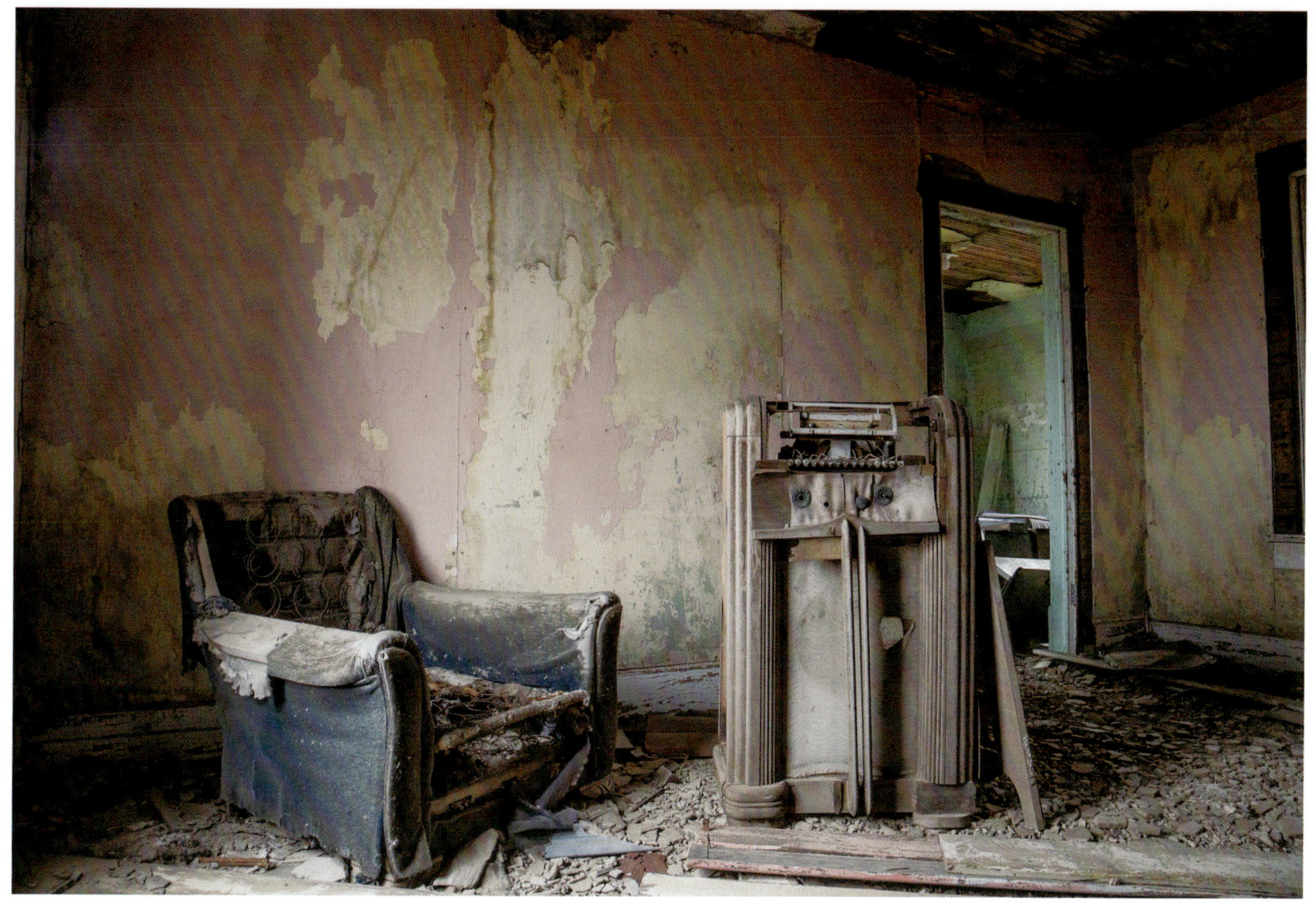

Interior, Williams County

Another property which we came across many years previously, this had changed little in the meantime. The colours, however, exuded a wonderful faded patina.

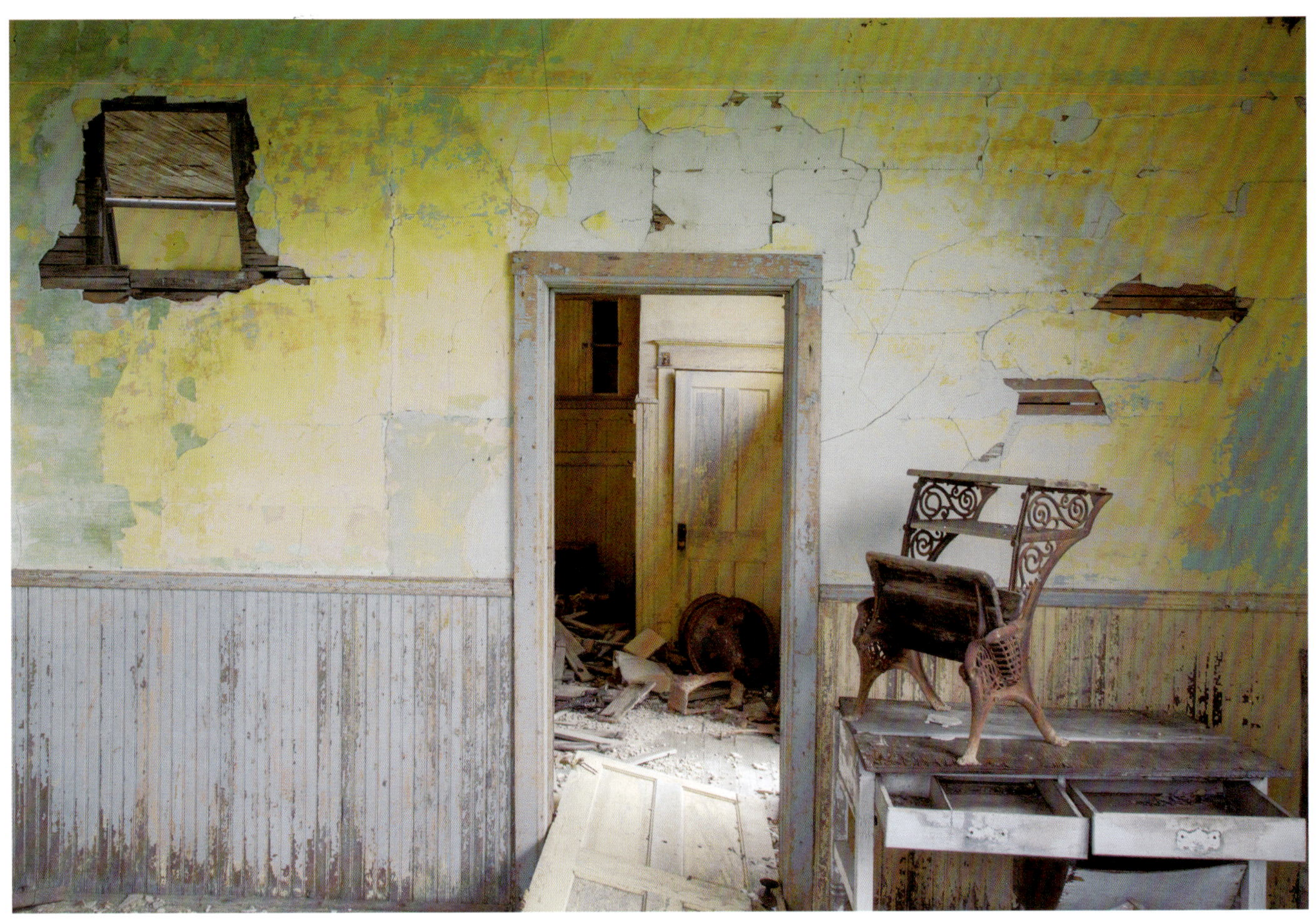

Interior of Griffin School

This is another building we had previously visited and photographed, however in this case we were witnessing noticeable changes. We gathered from a couple who lived nearby that ex-students were raiding the school and taking home old desks as keep-sakes.

Boarded up window, Scranton

Some of the properties we entered were so wrecked, that we wondered what was left to photograph. In this example, with much of the roof missing, shafts of light created interesting patterns.

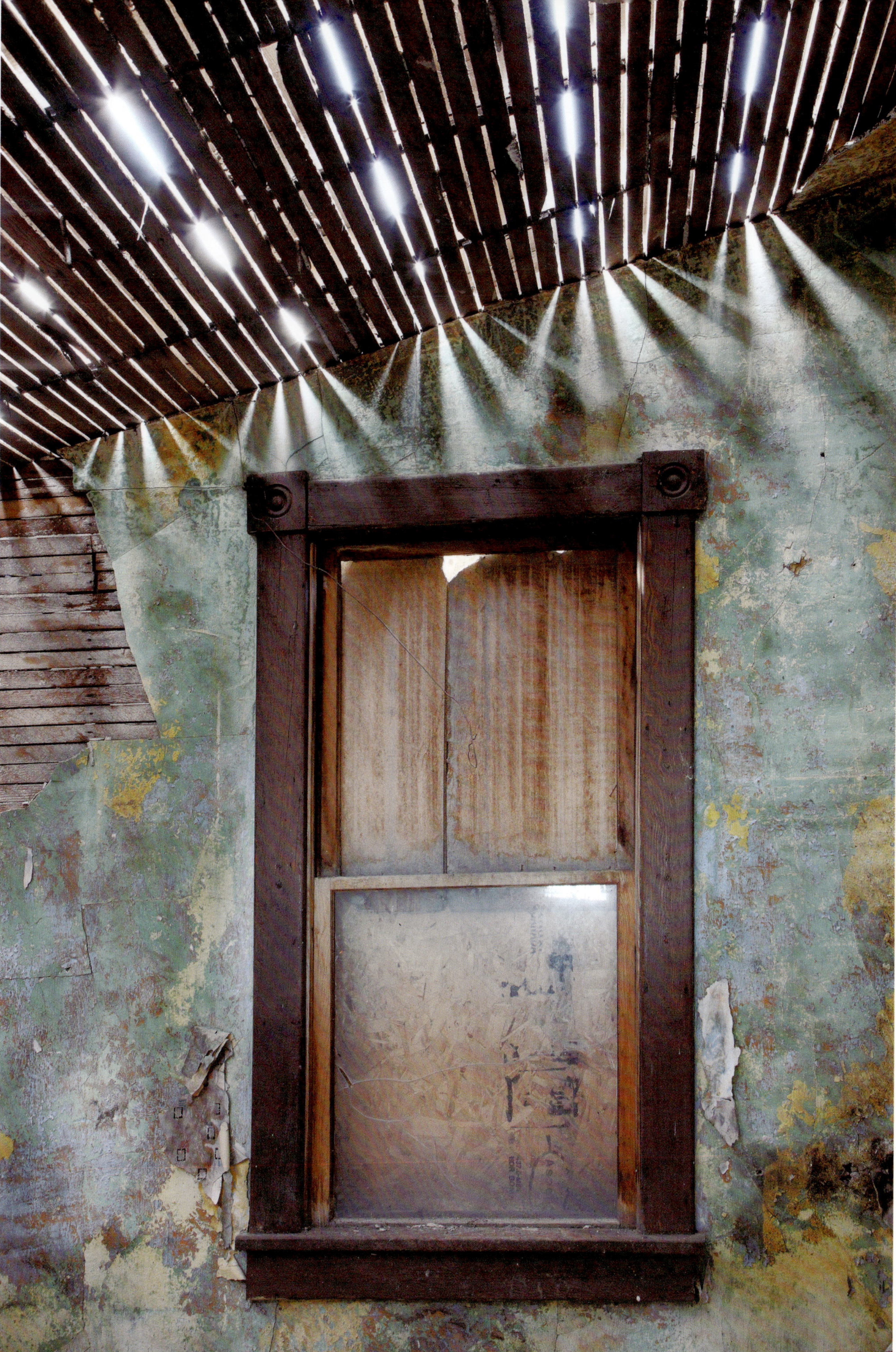

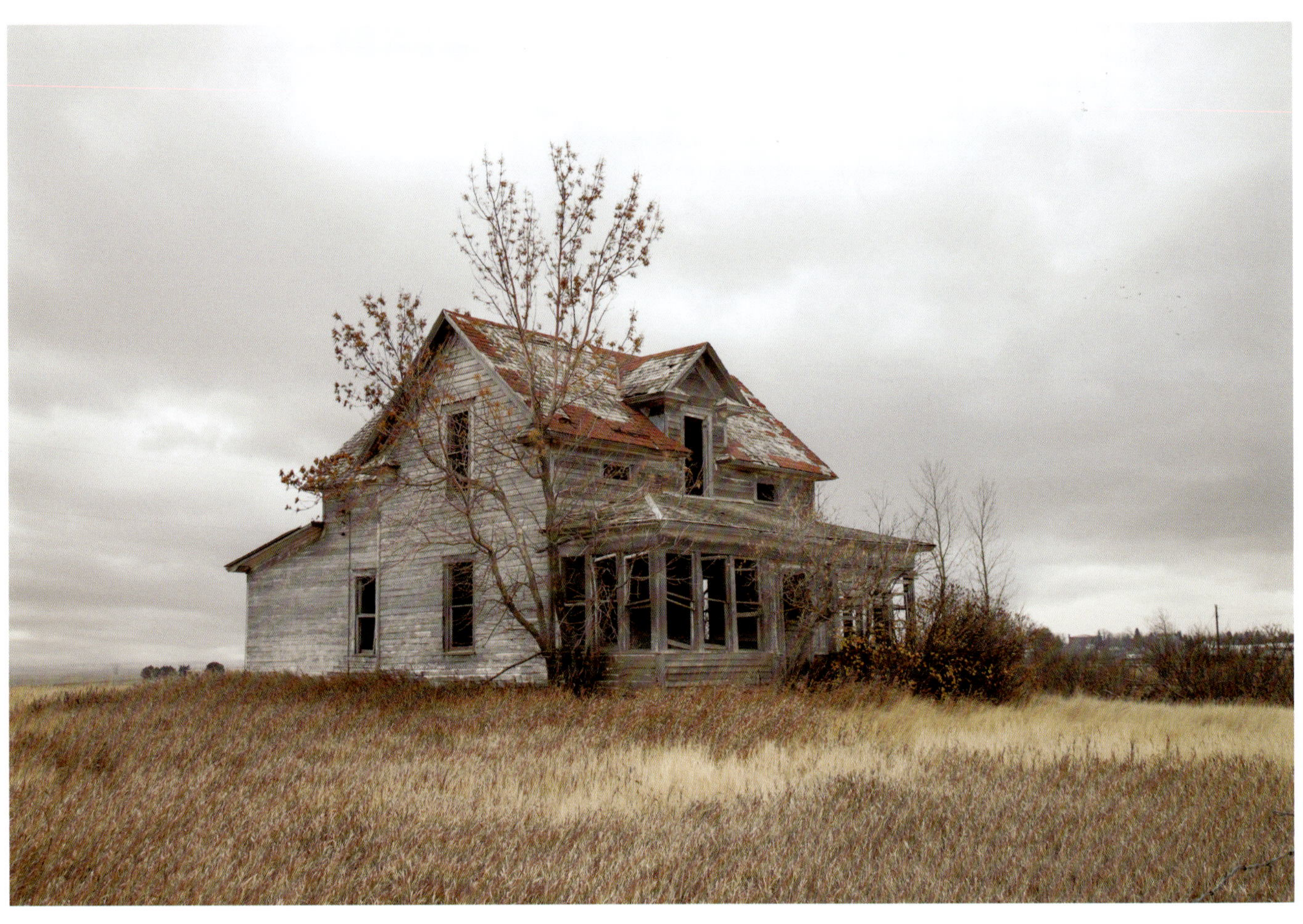

▲

Abandoned house

Once possibly a happy family home in a peaceful community, this house was deserted long before the current oil boom began.

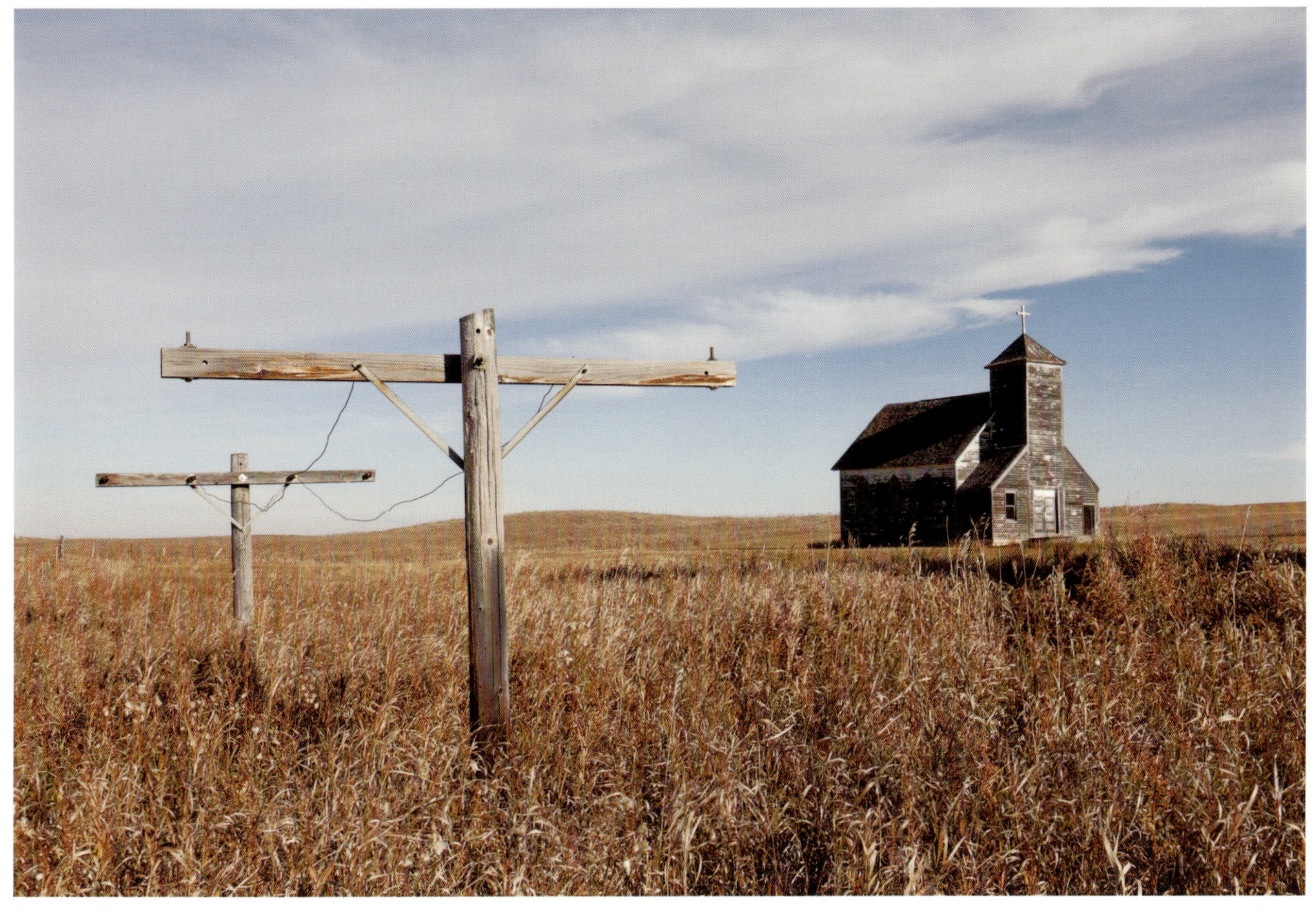

St John's Lutheran Church, Arena

Although it apparently closed formally for services in 1940, the church still stands proudly in Arena ghost town, where the only other buildings are an elevator and 2 houses.

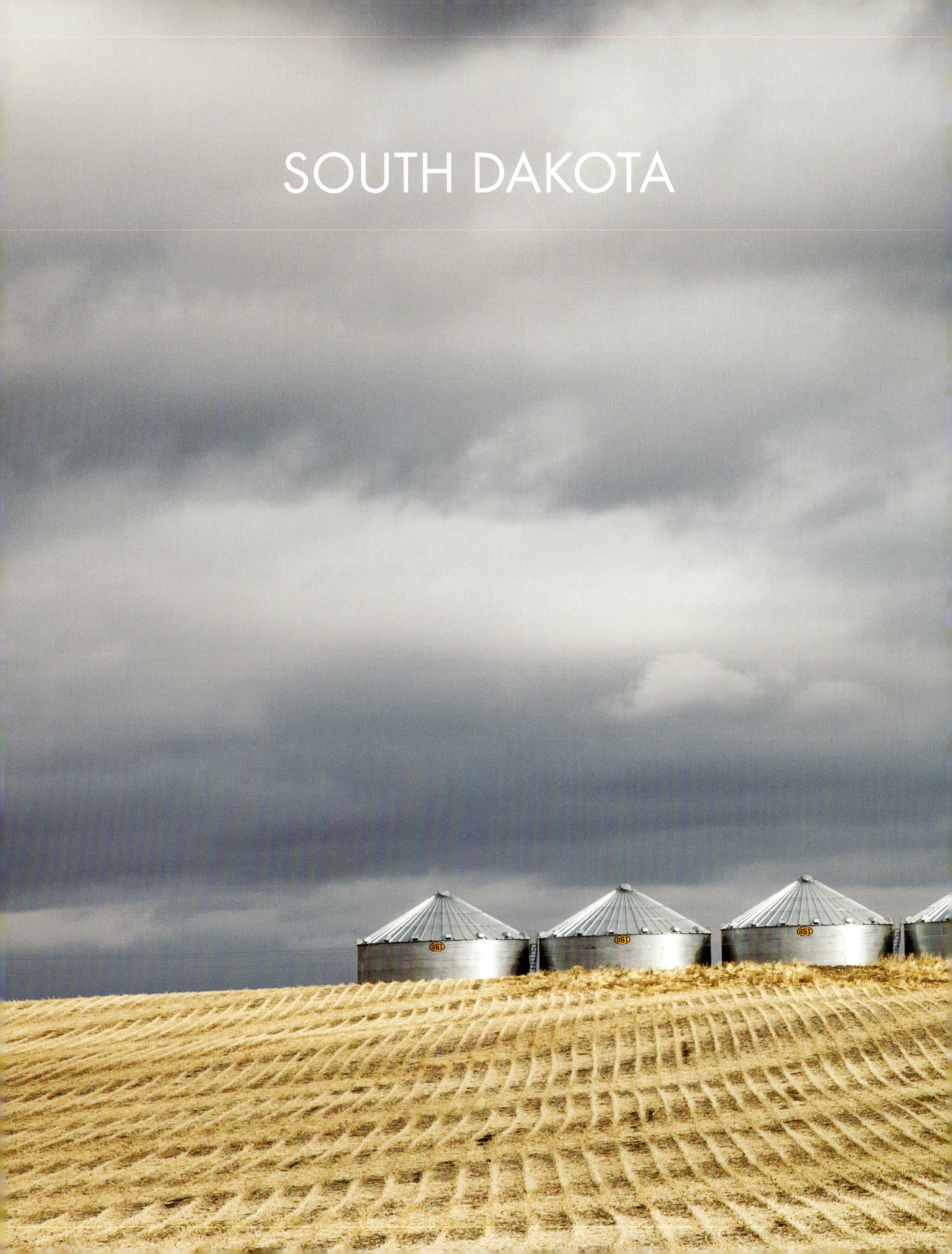

SOUTH DAKOTA

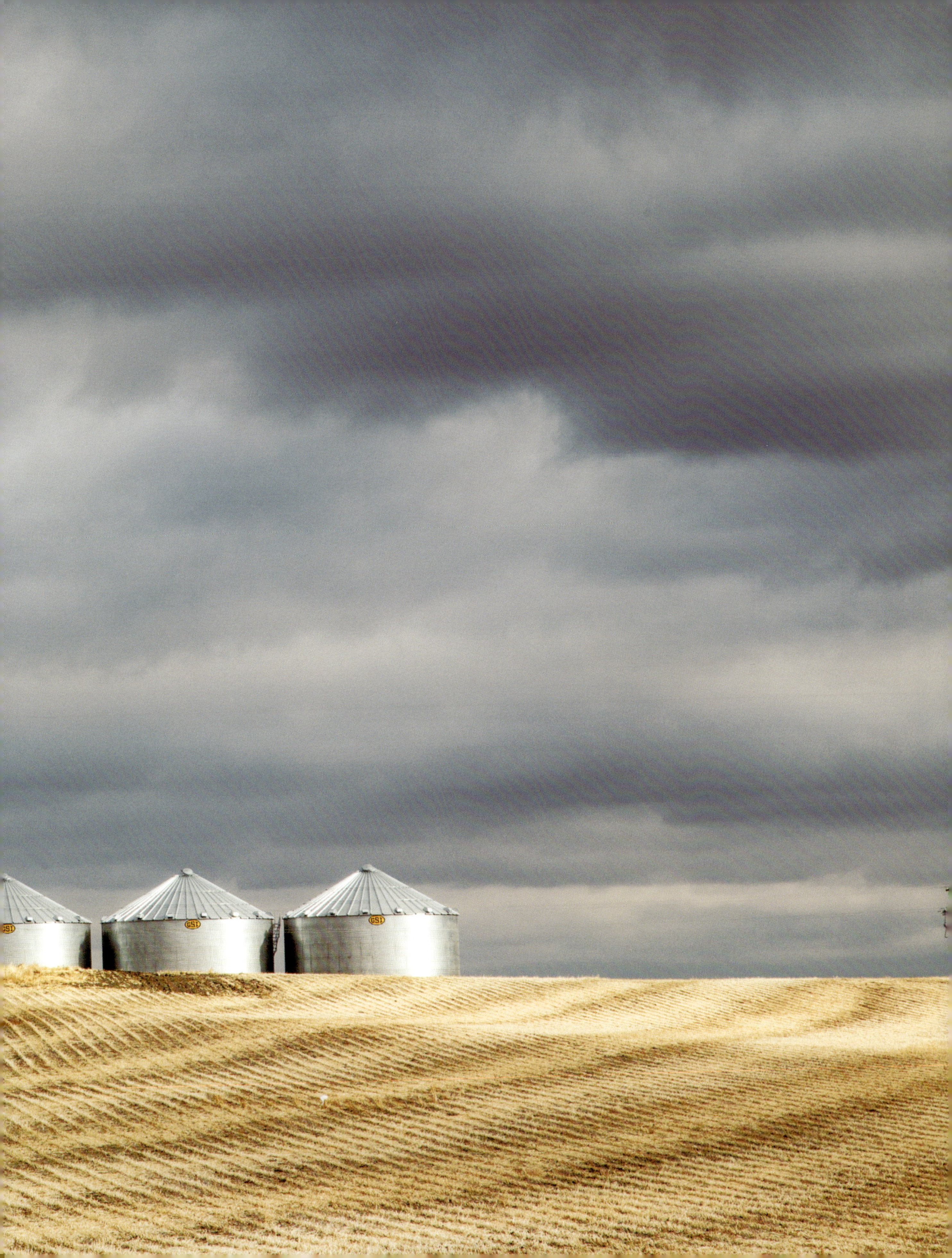

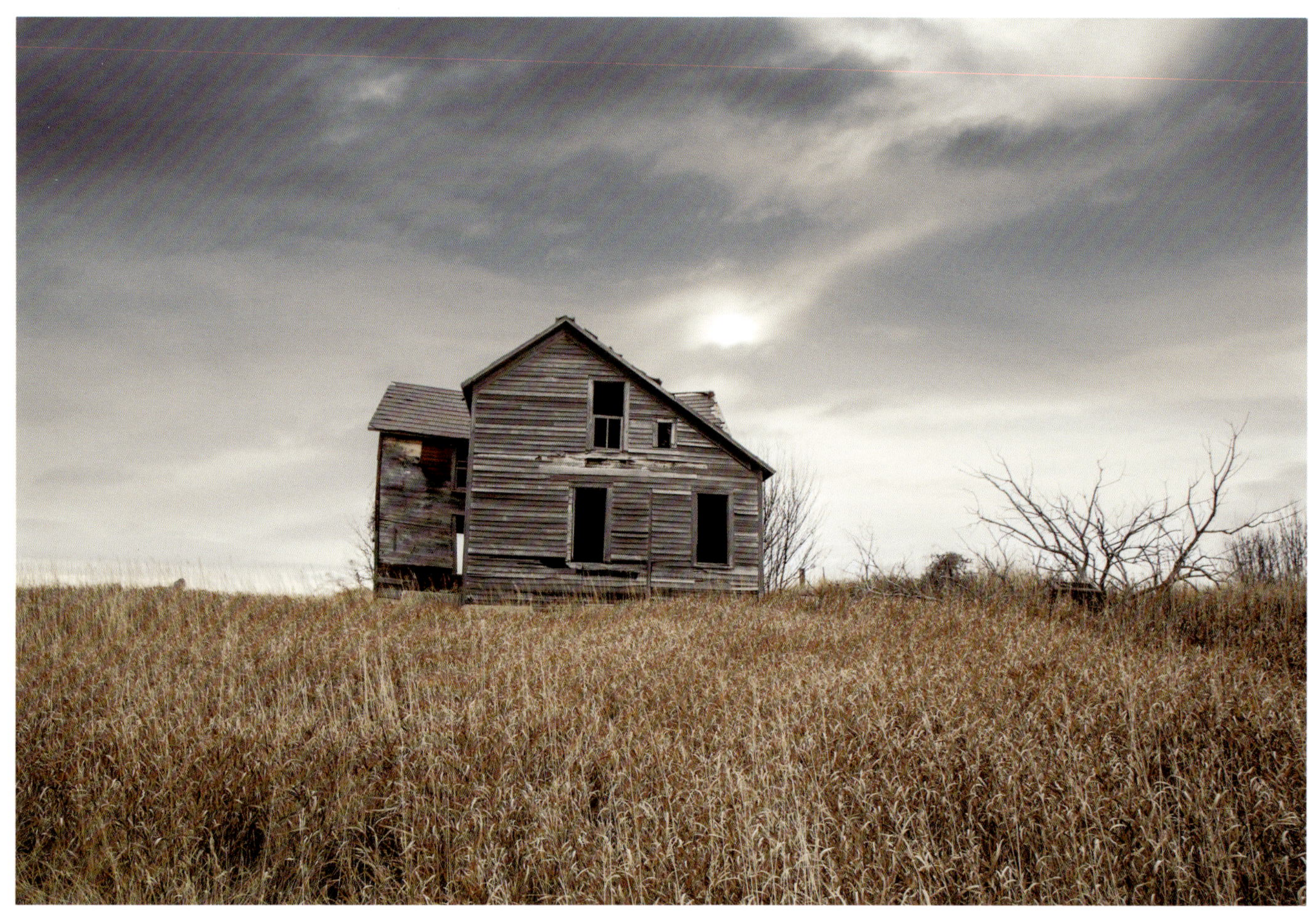

▲

Old Homestead, Okaton

*Most of the dwellings were timber-framed, which if they
are regularly maintained can last for years. Once they are
abandoned however, they very quickly fall into disrepair. As the
windows disappear, they are at the mercy of passing storms.*

▶

Discarded cowboy boots

*Many of the buildings we entered were astonishingly dark and initially
seeing any discarded objects is difficult, but as your eyes slowly adjust,
one begins to discover wonderfully iconic hidden gems.*

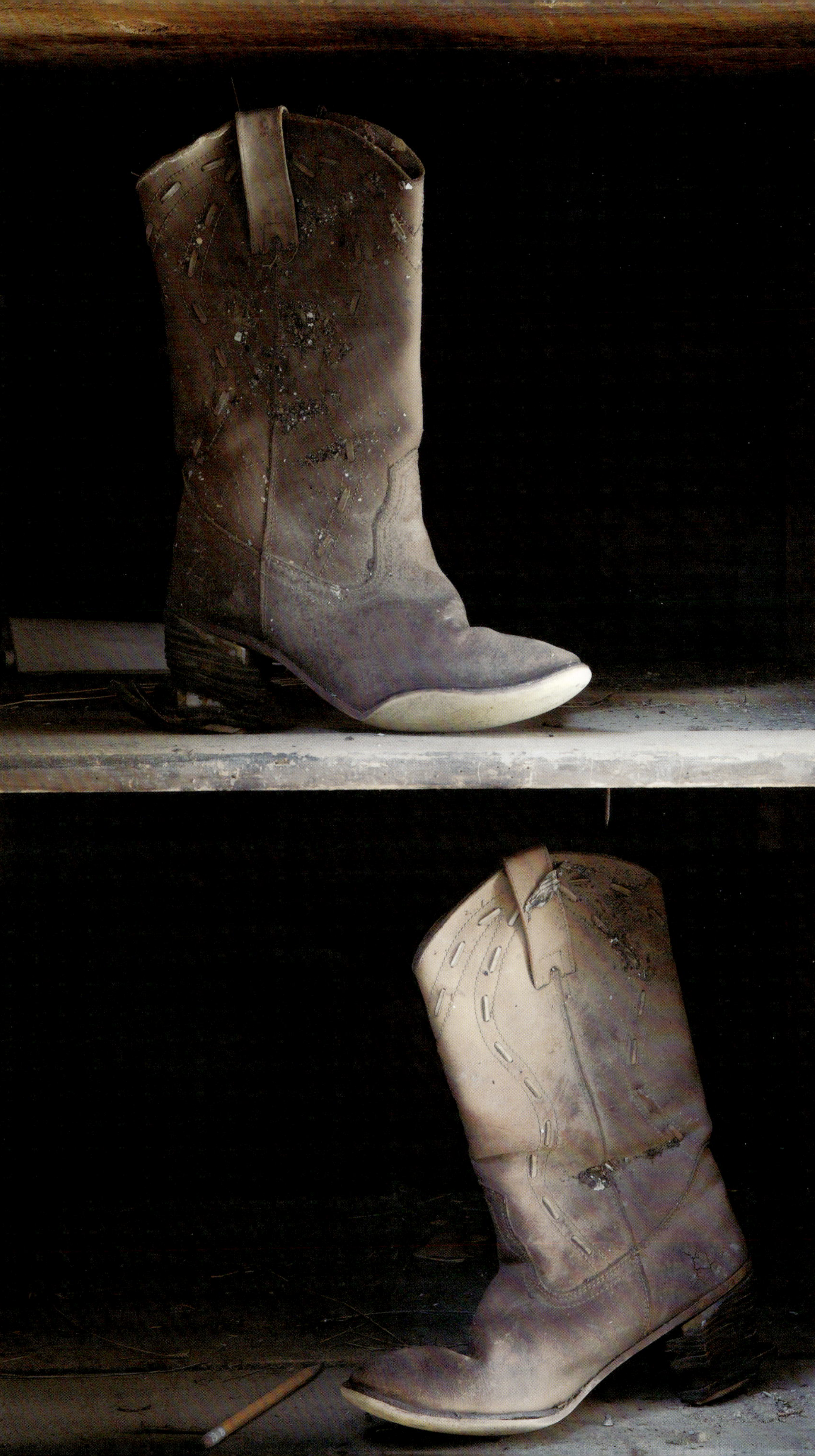

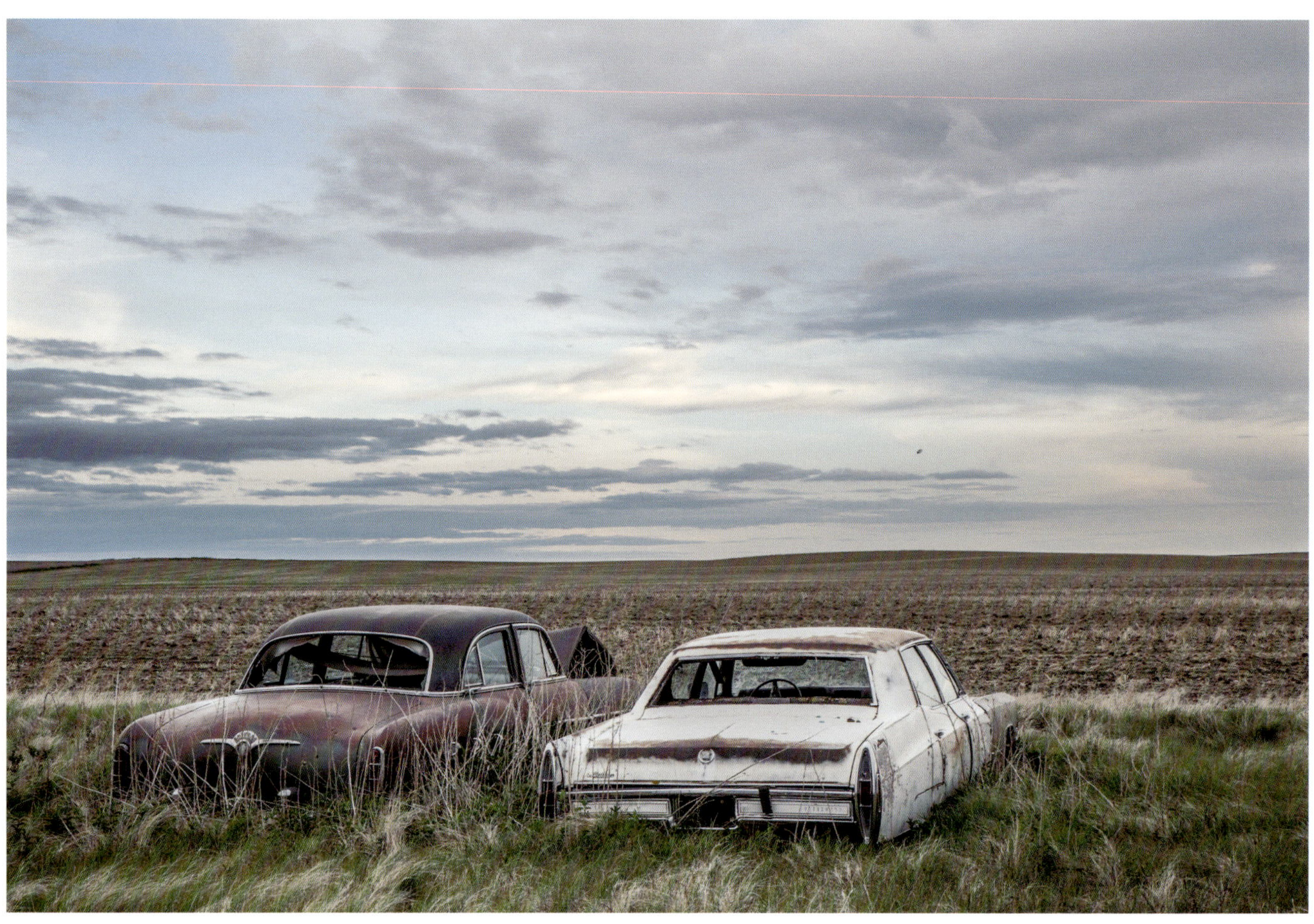

Two abandoned vehicles

Large towns on the prairies are very thinly spaced so when your vehicle does finally give up the ghost, there are no scrap-yards you can despatch it to. They are often abandoned in fields or along a quiet country track.

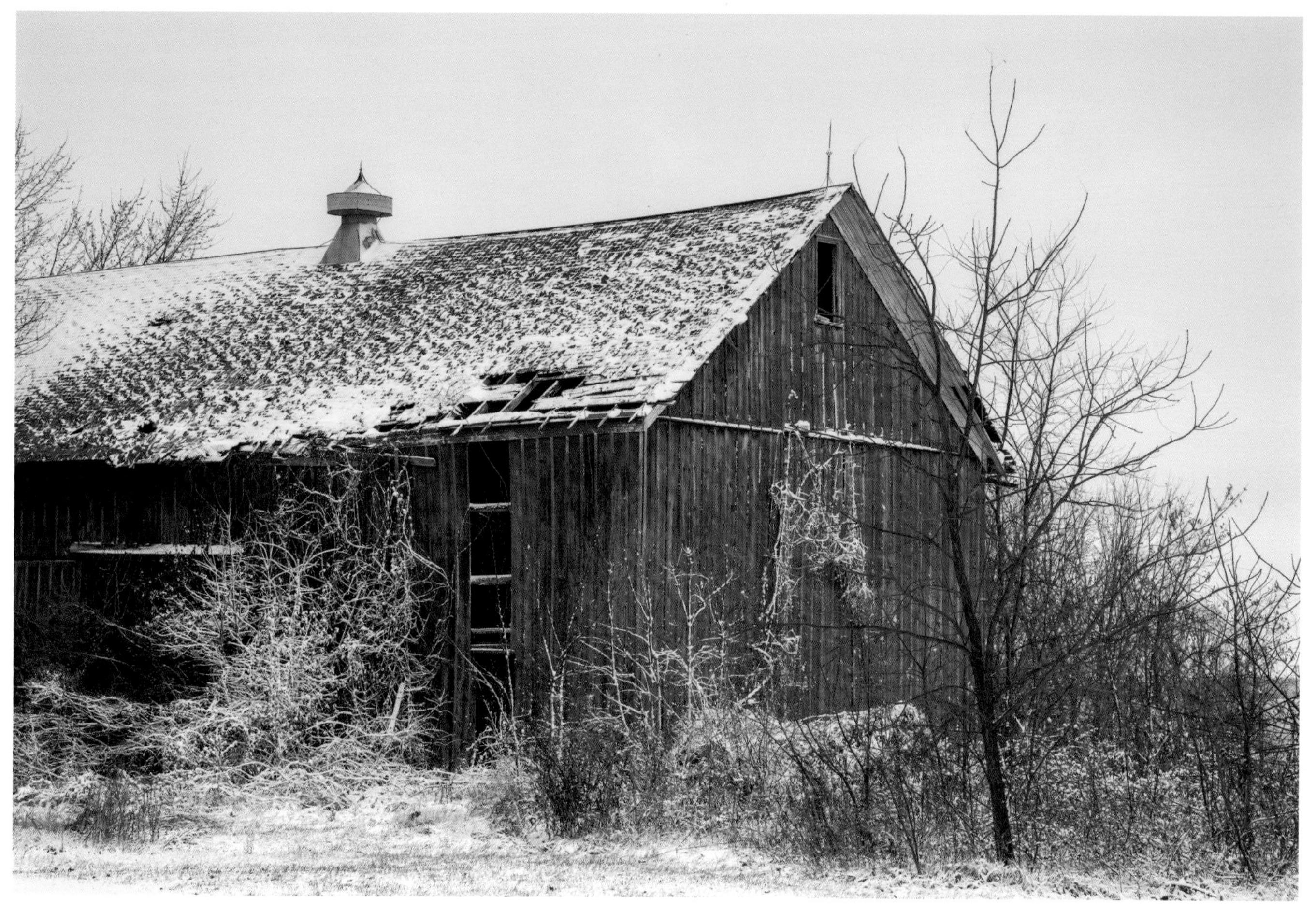

▲

Barn in snow

A feature which is often overlooked is just how extreme the weather can be on the High Plains; while is can be insufferably warm in summer, winter can arrive at the drop of a hat. These snows arrived in early November.

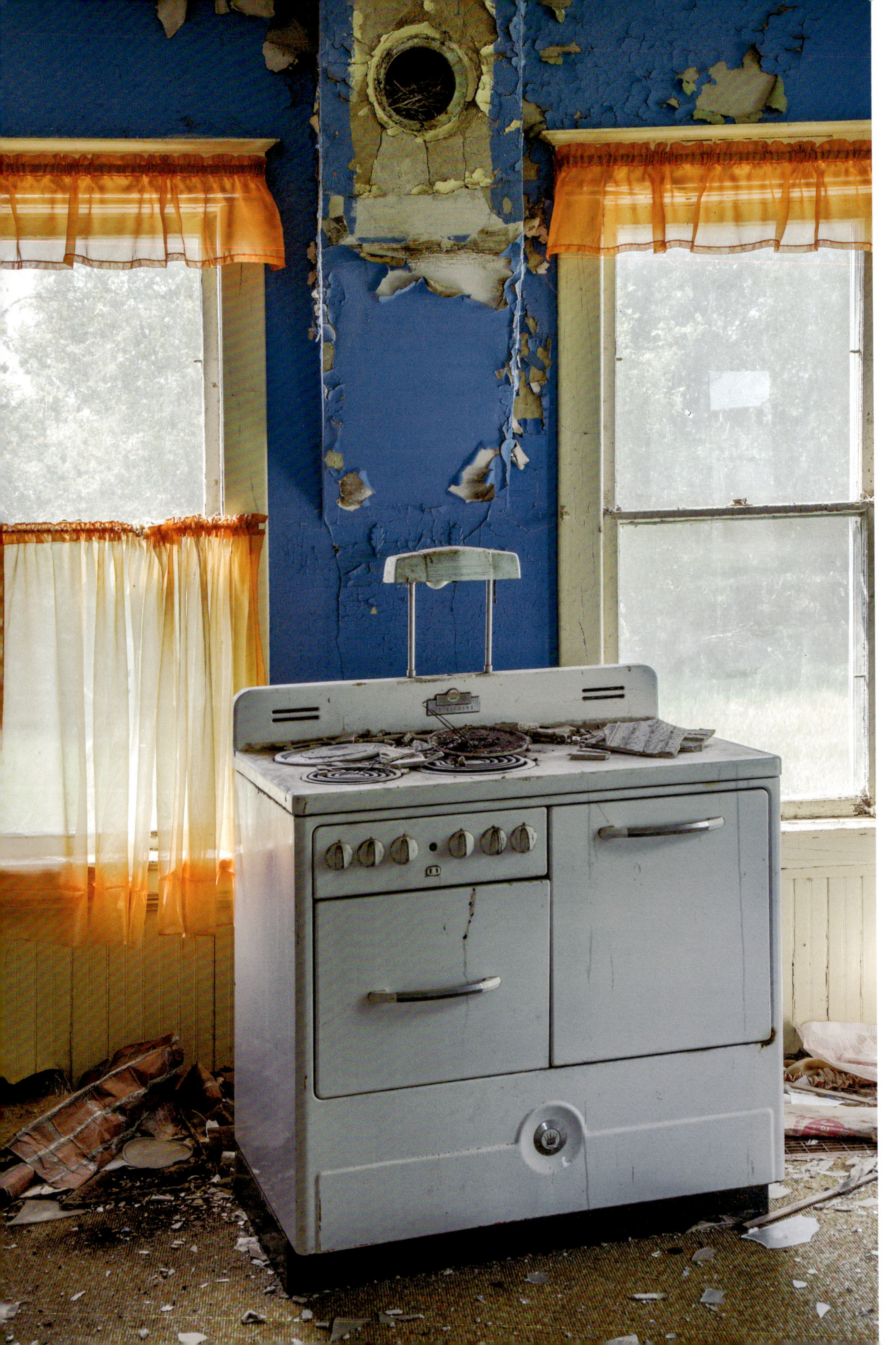

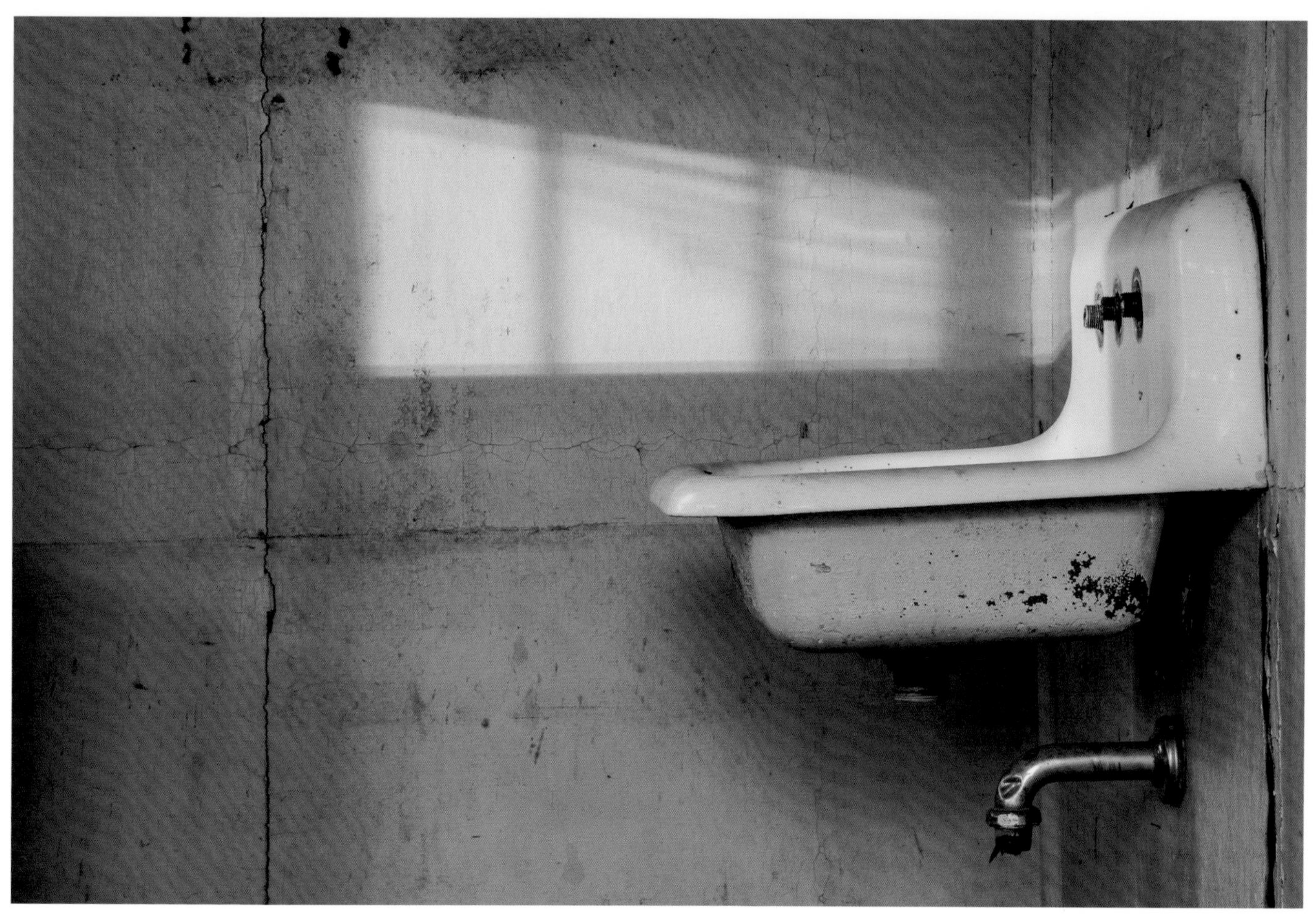

Washbasin

*With the outside light pouring into this building,
telling bits of detail are wonderfully illuminated.*

Interior with Frigidaire cooker

*It is easy to imagine that many of these
properties were abandoned decades ago, so it can
be quite sobering enter a building that was only
relatively recently vacated.*

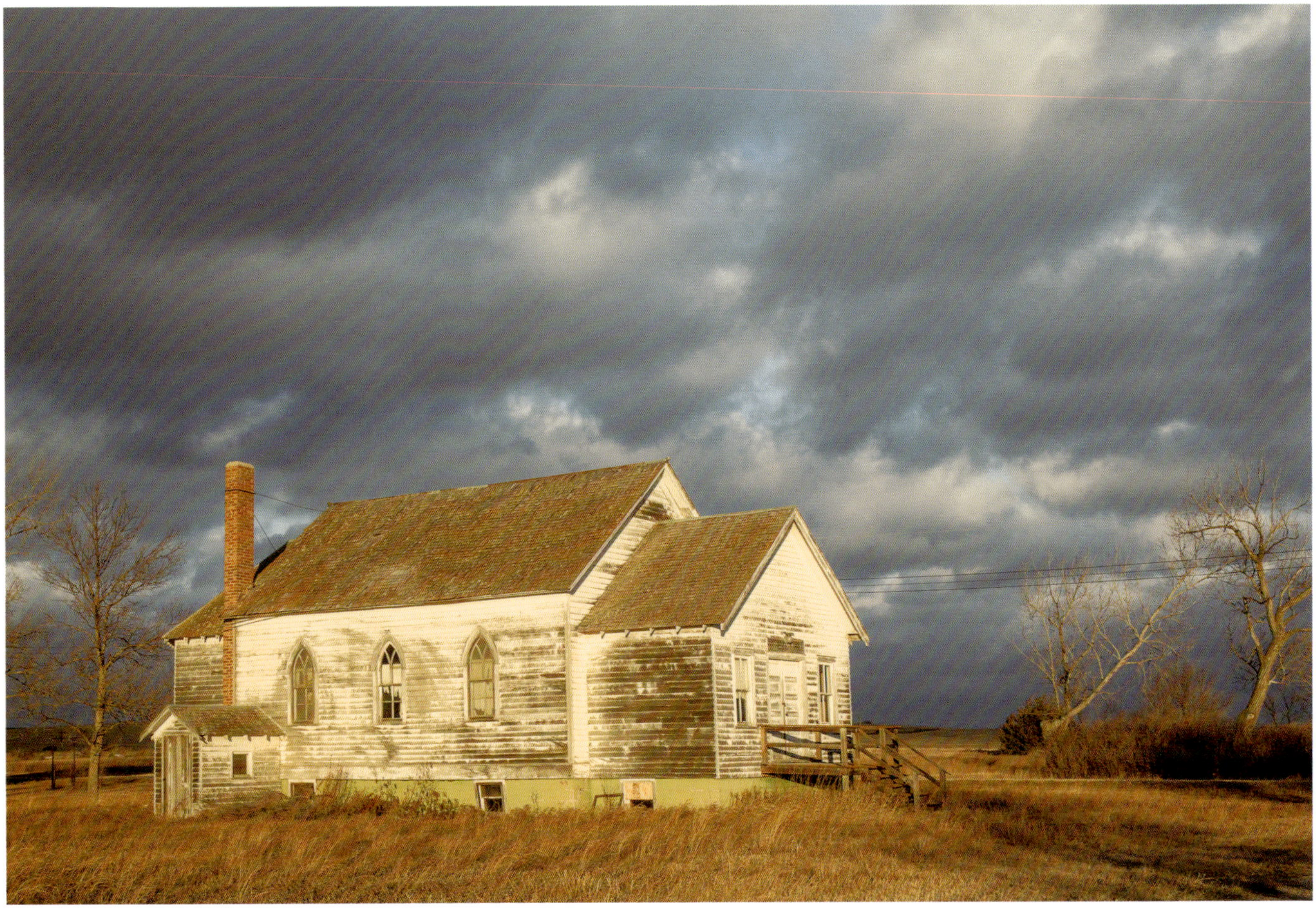

Artas City Hall

*Founded in 1901 by German-Russian settlers, the population
of Artas was recorded as 9 in the 2010 census.*

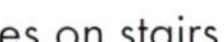

Shoes on stairs

*Occasionally one could experience the sense of a ghostly presence within
a deserted house: the shoes left on the staircase add to this impression.*

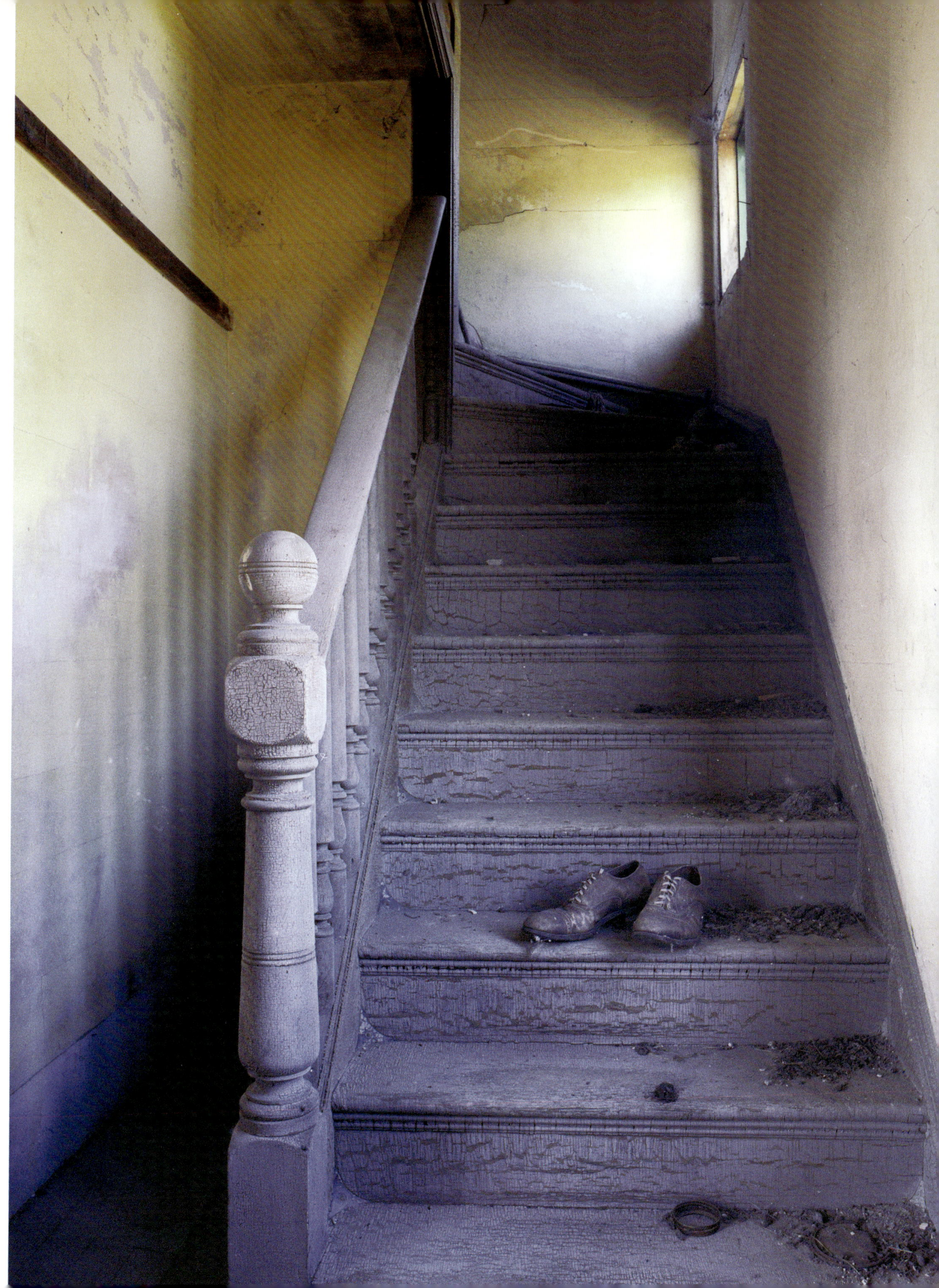

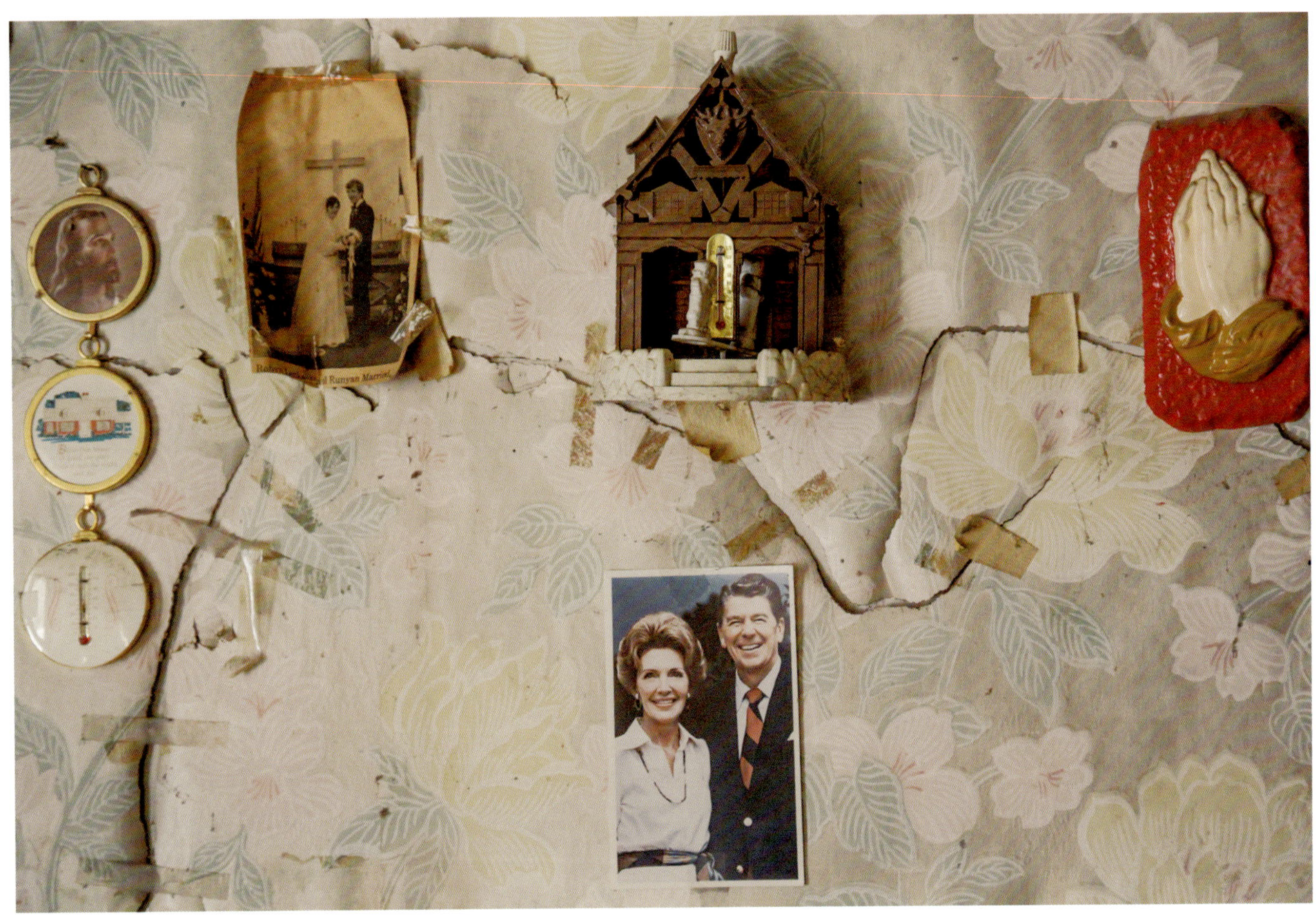

▲

A personal shrine

This sort of thing is extremely rare; most people when leaving their homes take their photographs with them. The occupants of this property had created this little shrine which certainly gives us an insight into their politics and values.

▶

Detail from mail van

Again, the dry climate tends to preserve colours and details in old abandoned vehicles: the design here is reminiscent of an abstract painting.

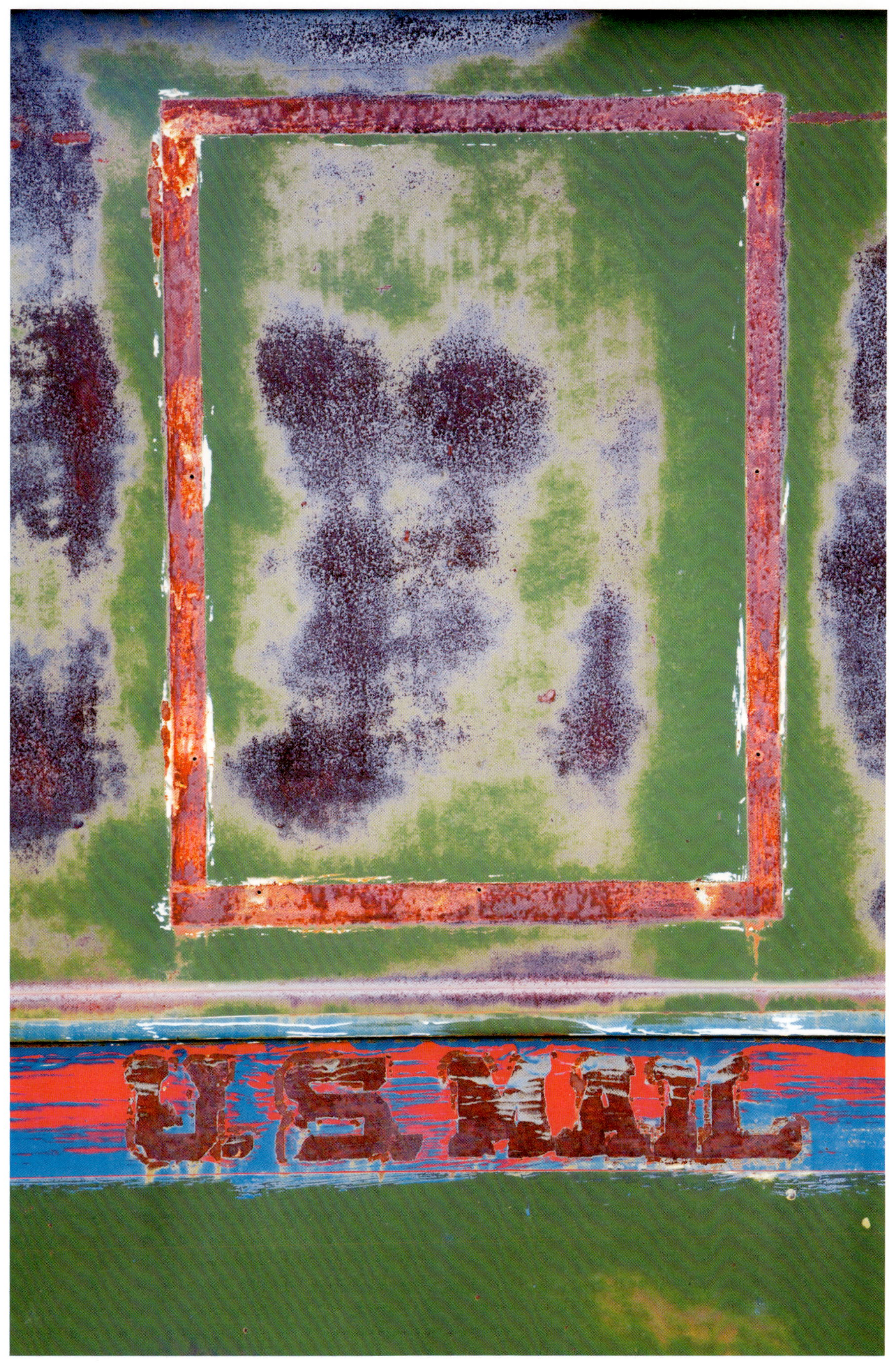
U.S. MAIL

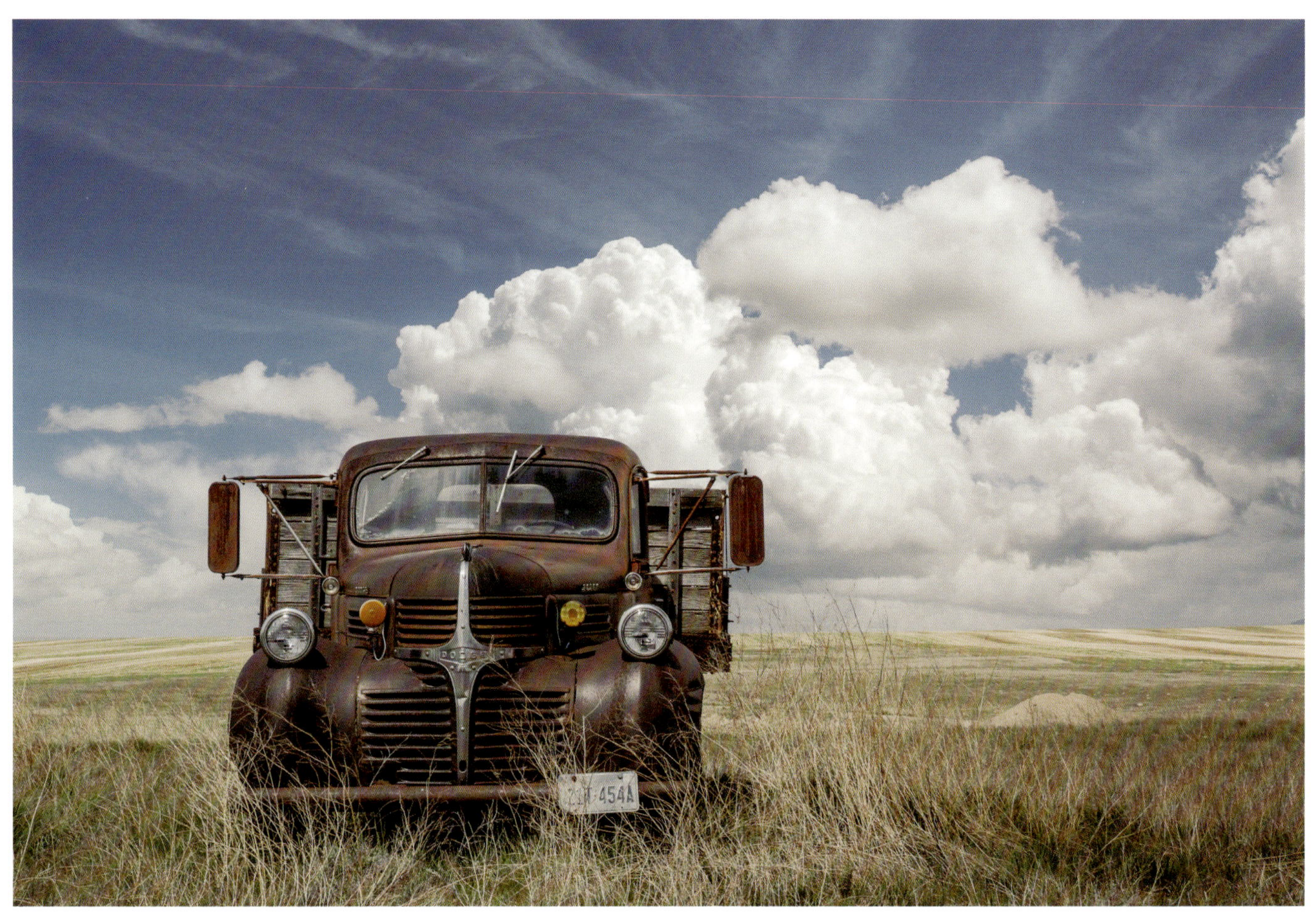

An abandoned Dodge pickup

As a consequence of the relatively dry climate, (which of course is why so many farmers were forced to give up), the numerous vehicles littering the fields survive relatively intact.

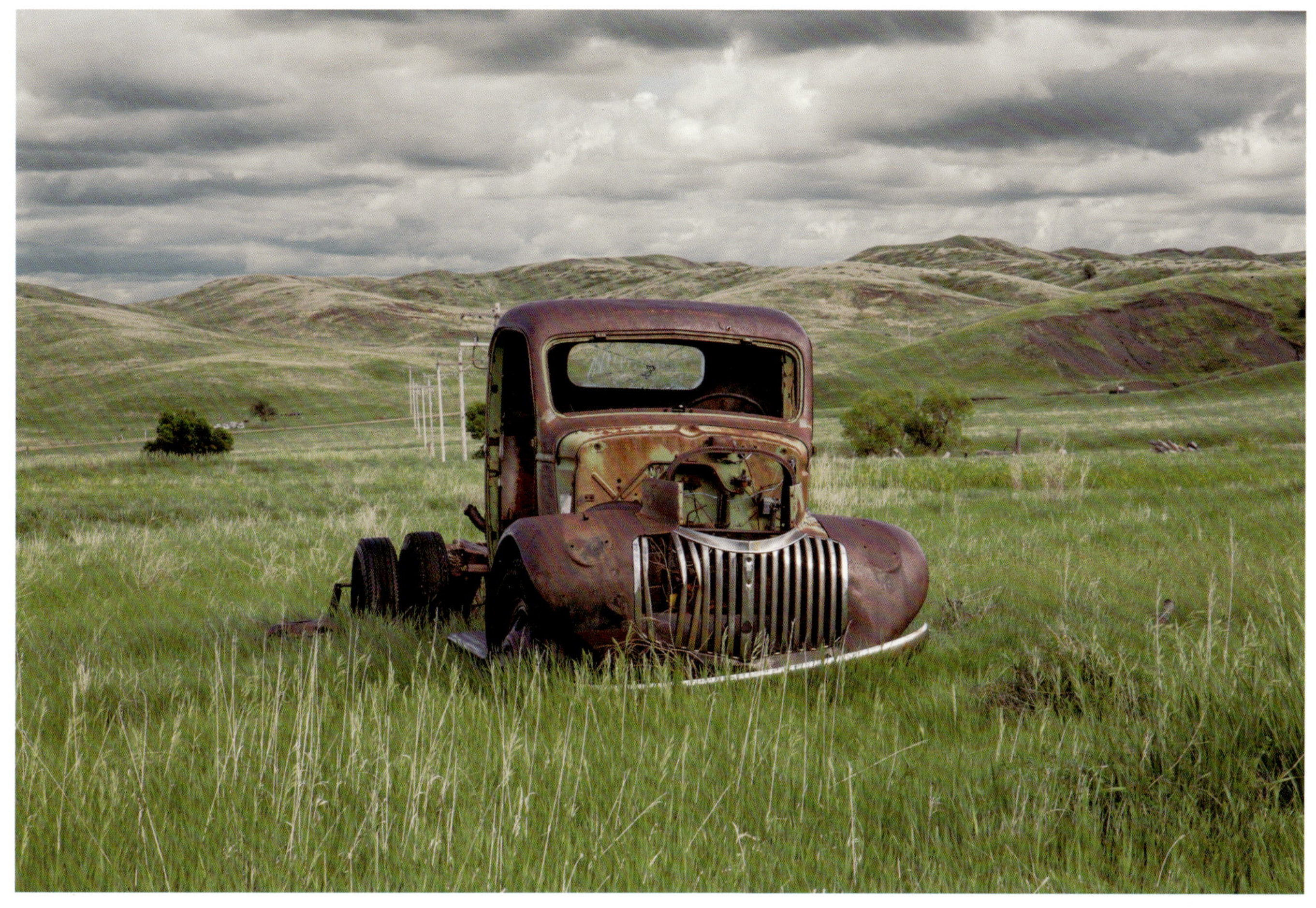

▲

Abandoned 1940s pickup

The community, now a virtual ghost town, enjoyed a more favourable situation than many others, being protected from snowstorms and strong winds by its location in a beautiful valley. Each abandoned vehicle represents the hopes and aspirations of the families that once owned them.

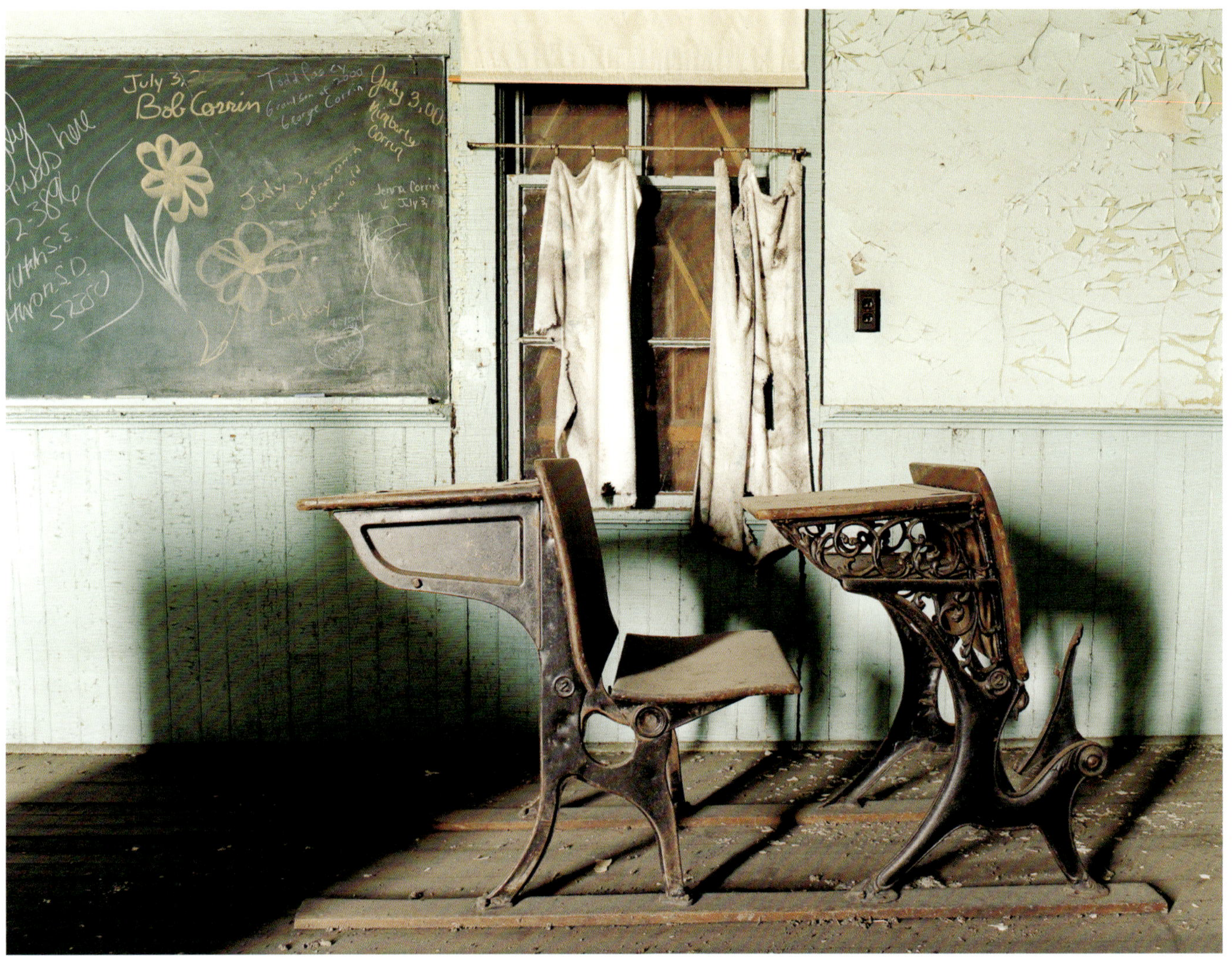

▲

Corrin School, near Miller

*These old wrought iron school desks could well be about 100
years old and are now extremely sought after.*

▶

Green chair and hat

*Due in part to the laws governing trespass, very few of the properties
we entered had been visited by anyone else. These buildings would
often become a refuge for wild animals as the paw marks on this
chair would indicate; we suspect a raccoon had recently passed by.*

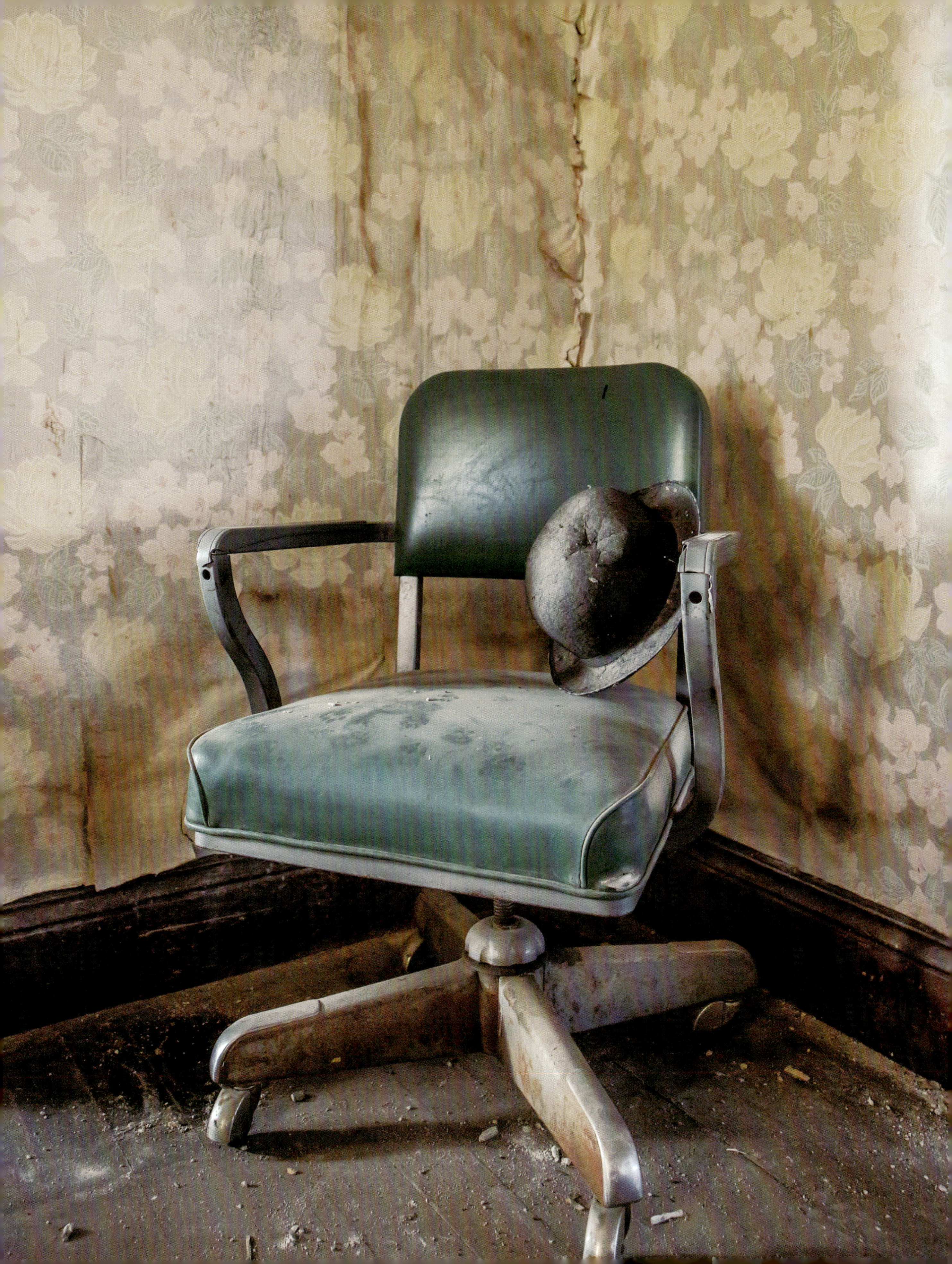

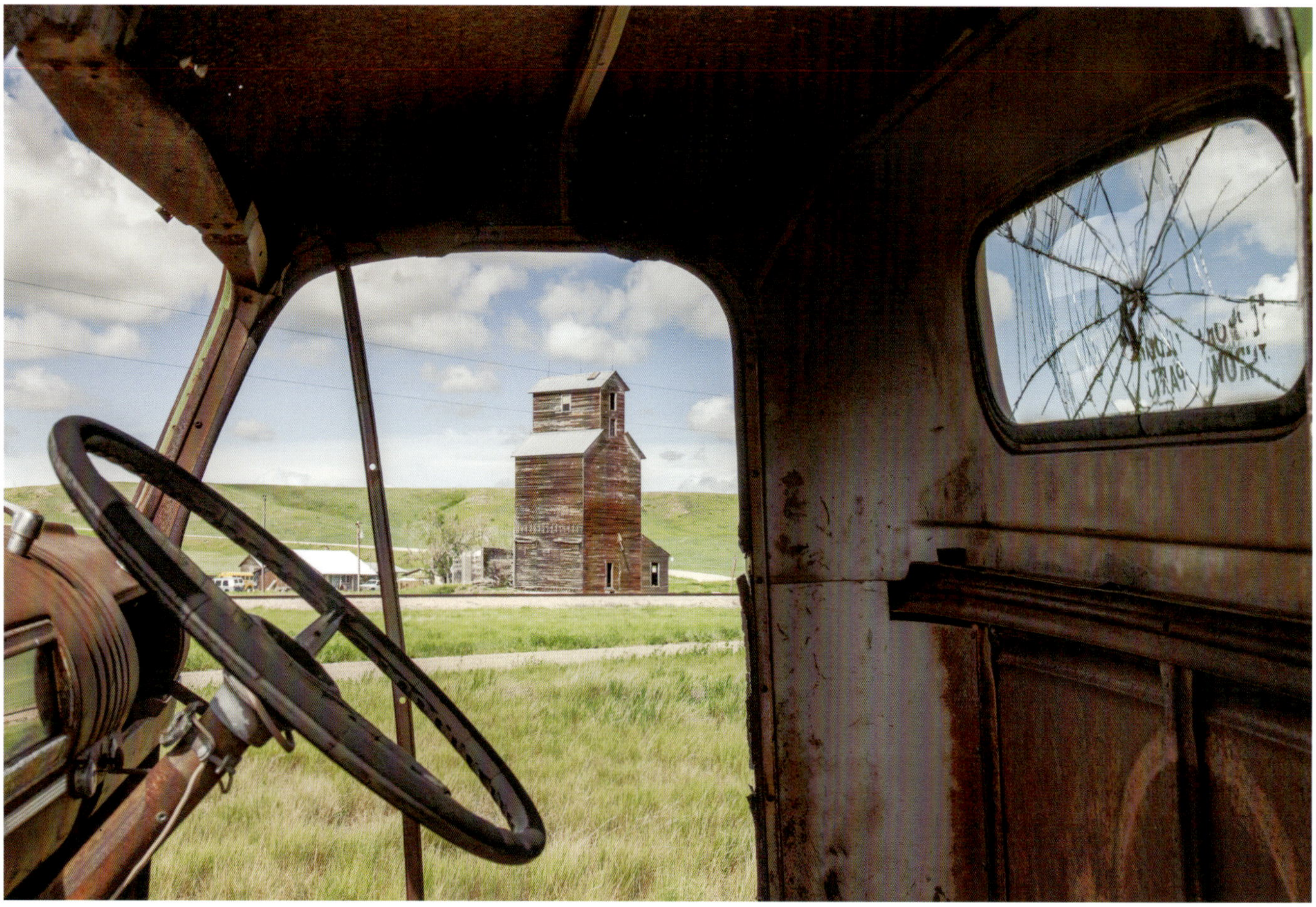

View of lone elevator, Owanka

Once a thriving community in the early 20th century due to the railroad, Owanka gradually declined due to a series of unrelated events, including being bypassed by a major road some 5 miles north.

Chair and discarded baseball cap

Part of the fascination of entering an abandoned building is that you discover small, yet iconic scraps which help to define the area you are travelling through.

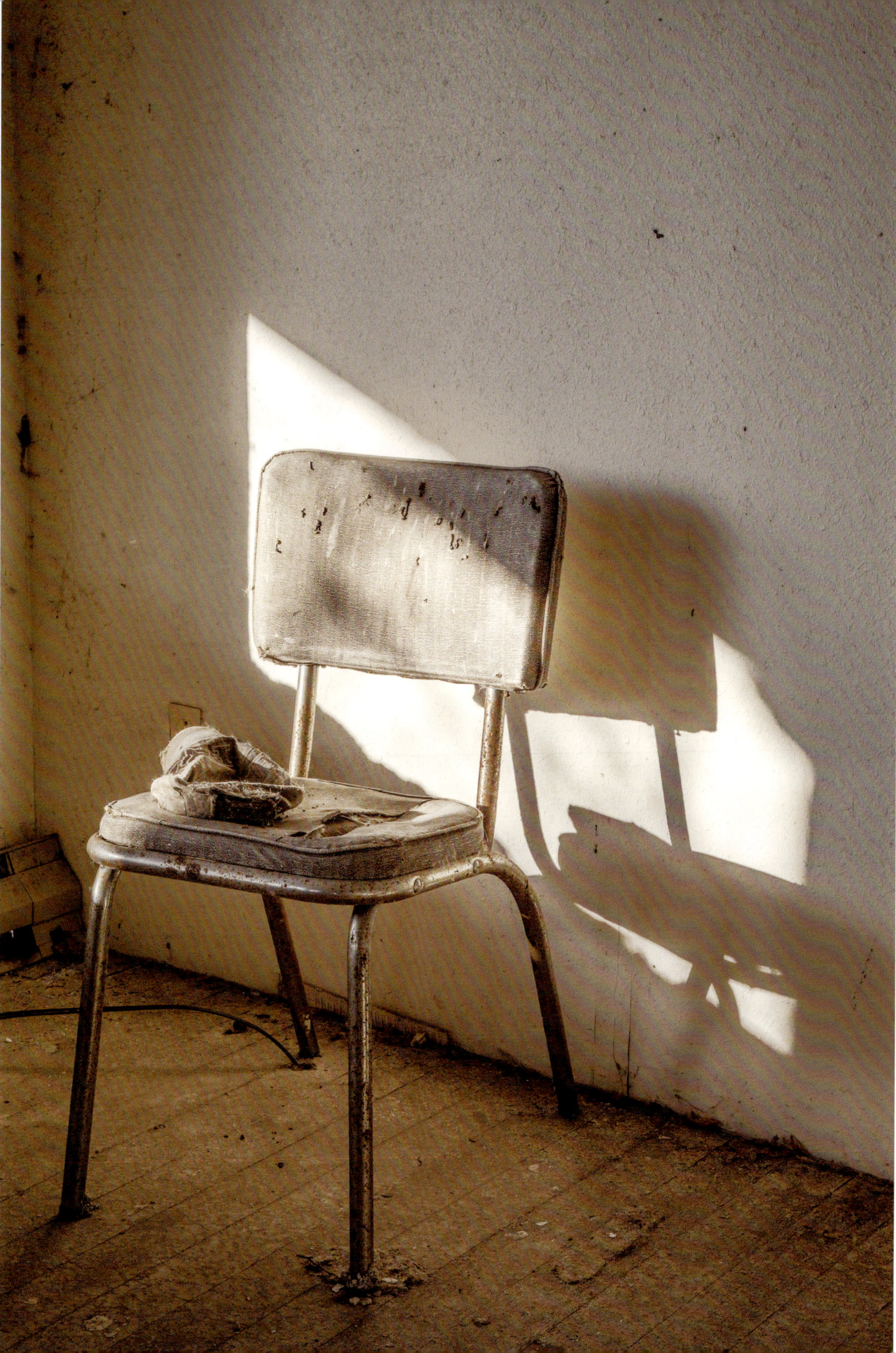

CENTRAL PLAINS

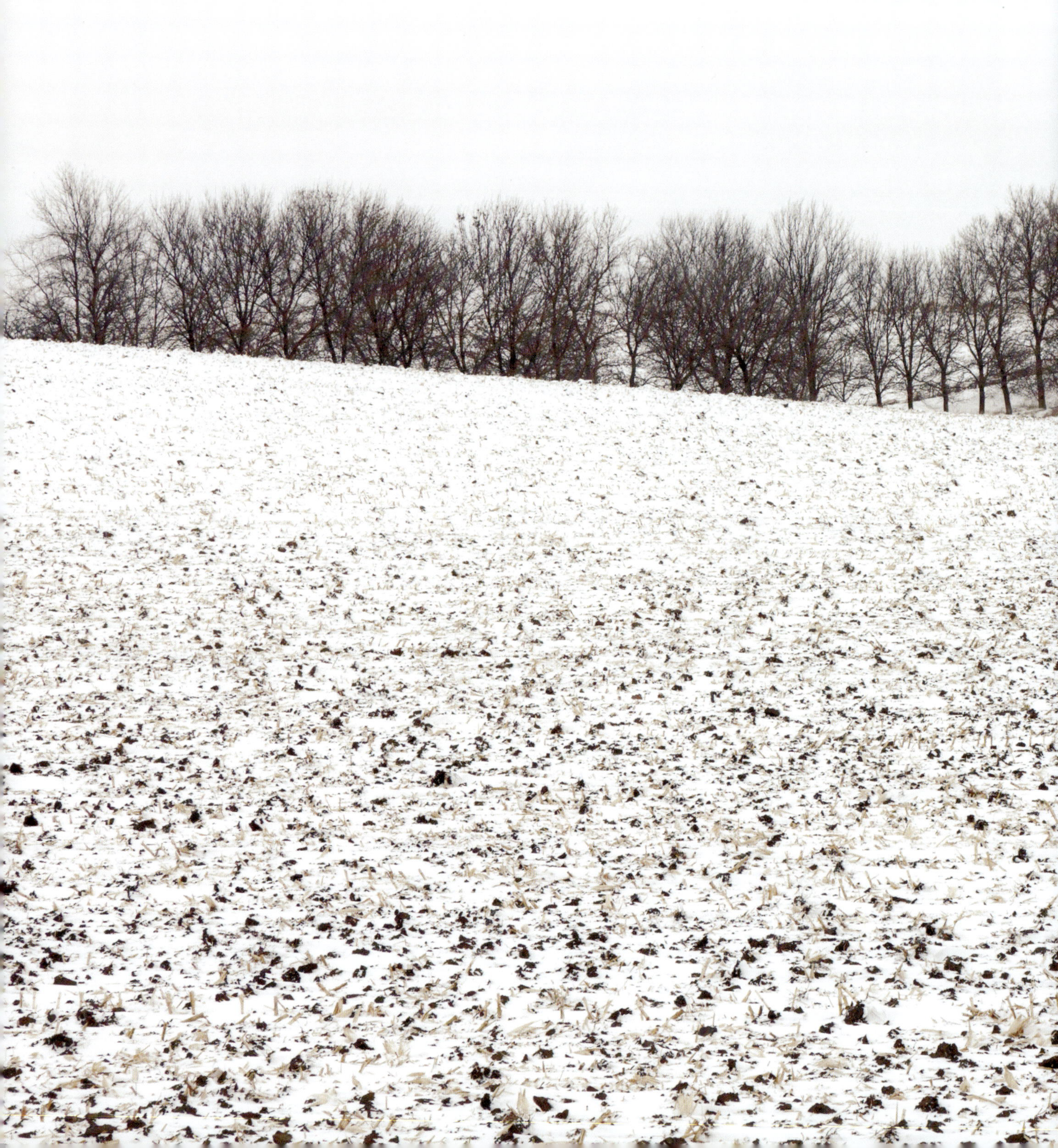

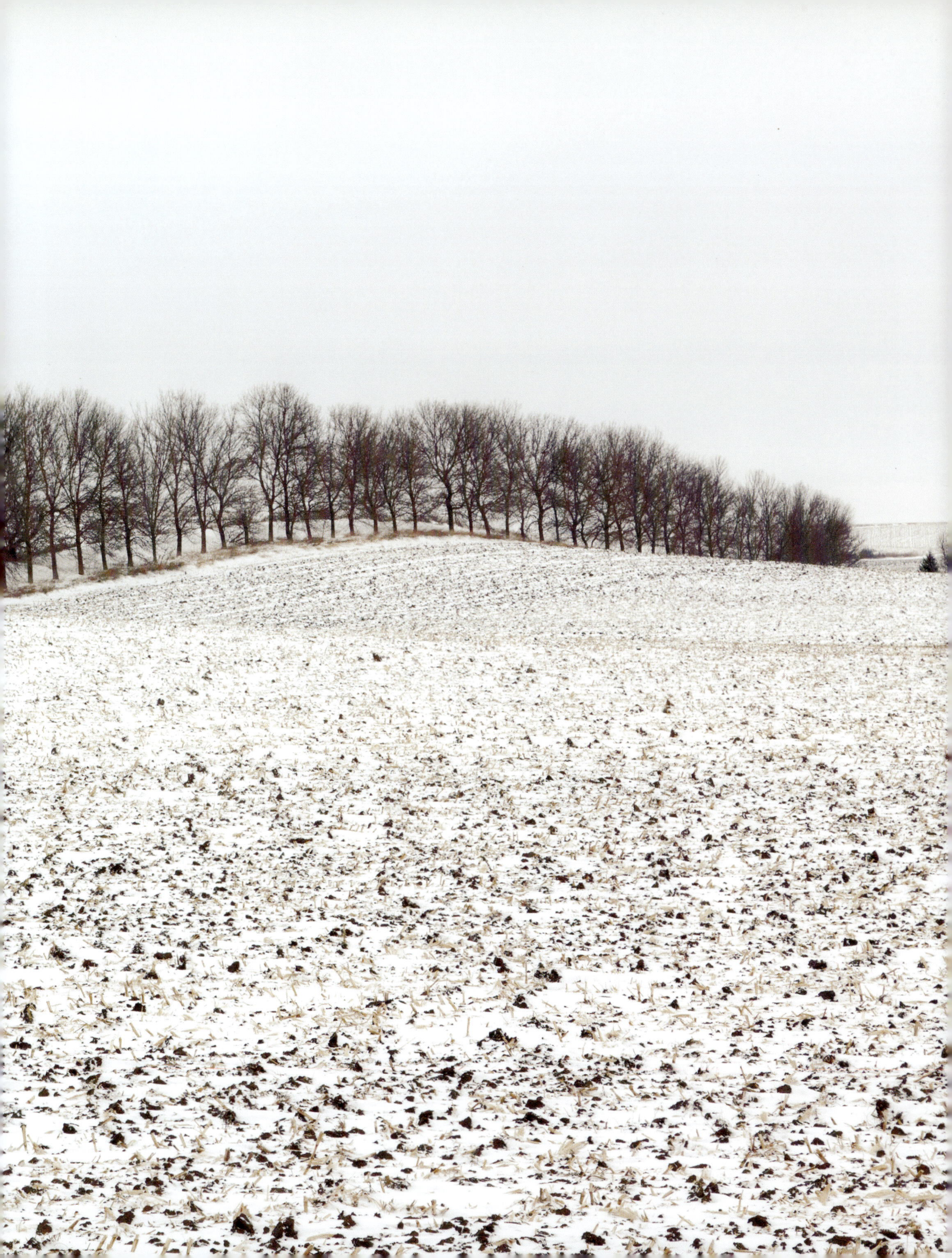

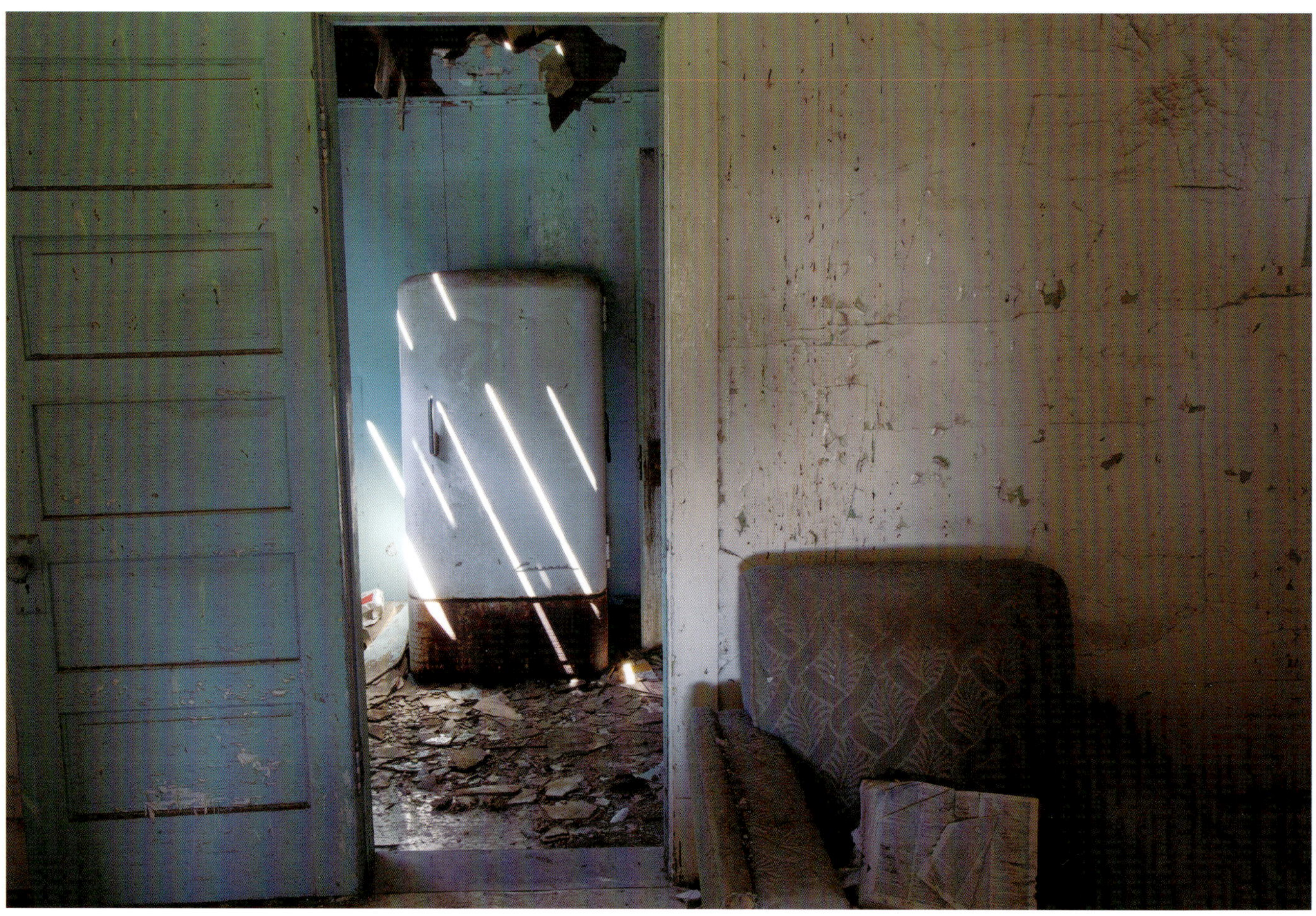

Chair with fridge in background

While the furniture remains generally intact, the forces of nature are having an impact on the general fabric of the building which is gradually crumbling.

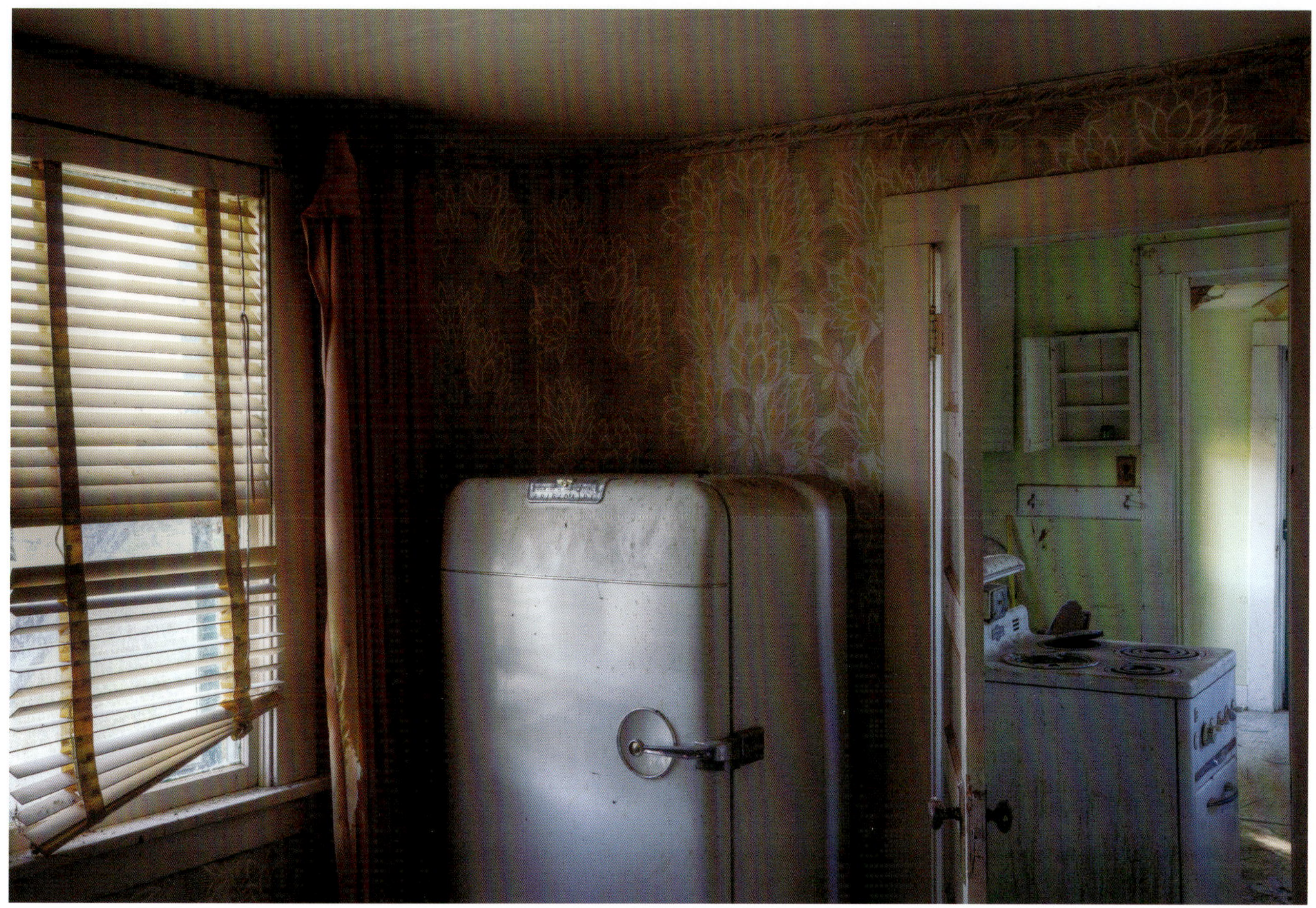

Kitchen

What continues to amaze us is just how intact some of the buildings we visited remain. One senses that simply by reconnecting to the utilities, it would be possible to live in this house once again.

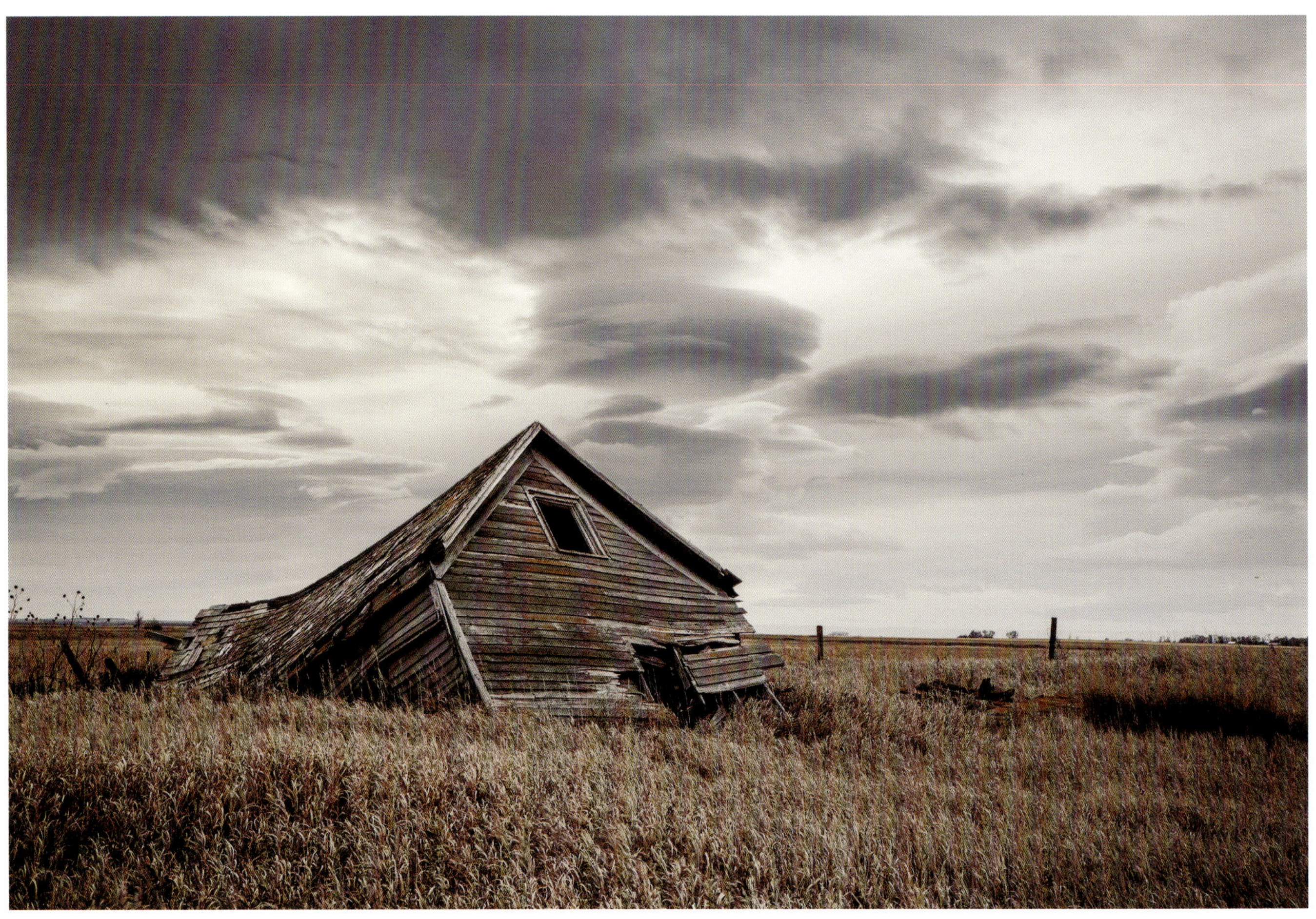

▲

Collapsed house on the plain, Minnesota

*Once a property had been abandoned, it didn't take too long for
a sequence of baking hot summers and the cold winds of winter
to attack its structure. Factor in the occasional tornado, and such
scenes become common-place.*

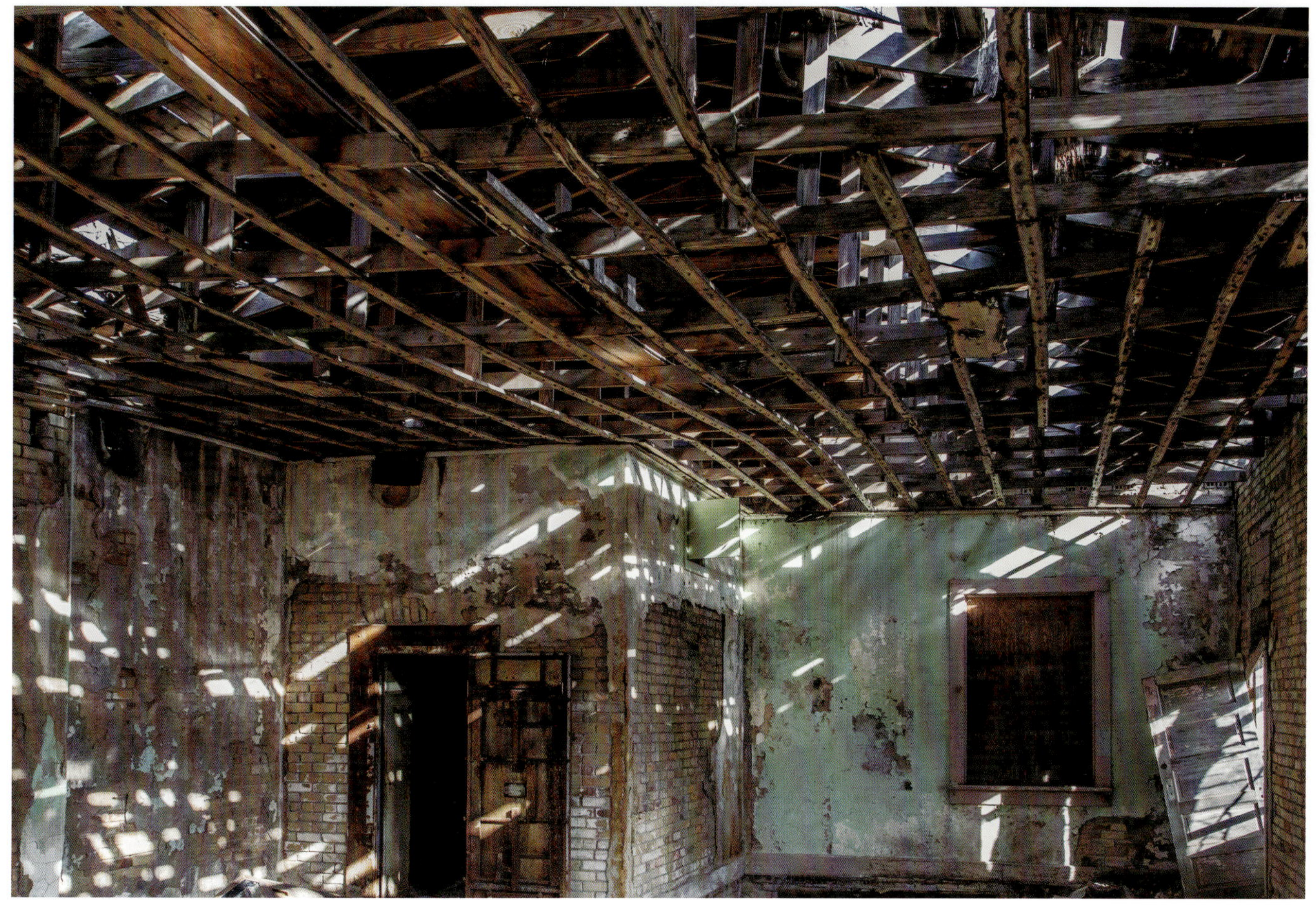

Empty bank

Banks tended to be local institutions, so once a community folded, then so indeed did the bank. The open door to the vaults can be seen in the bottom left of the picture.

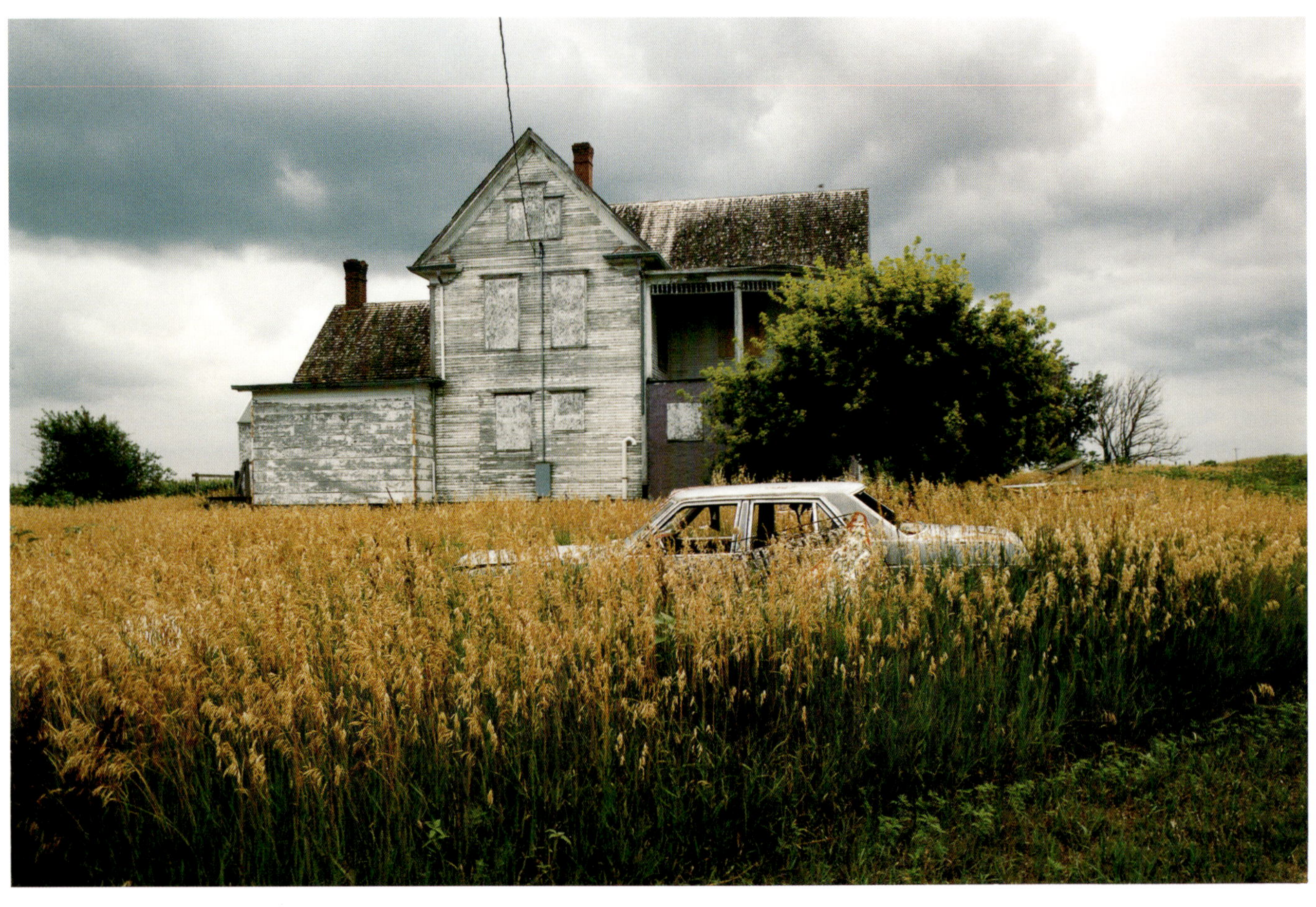

House near Ord, Nebraska

One wonders what the history of this fine old house might be and what made its occupants leave.

Solitary armchair, Angora, Nebraska

A single armchair would often be the only remaining piece of furniture – usually placed by a window.

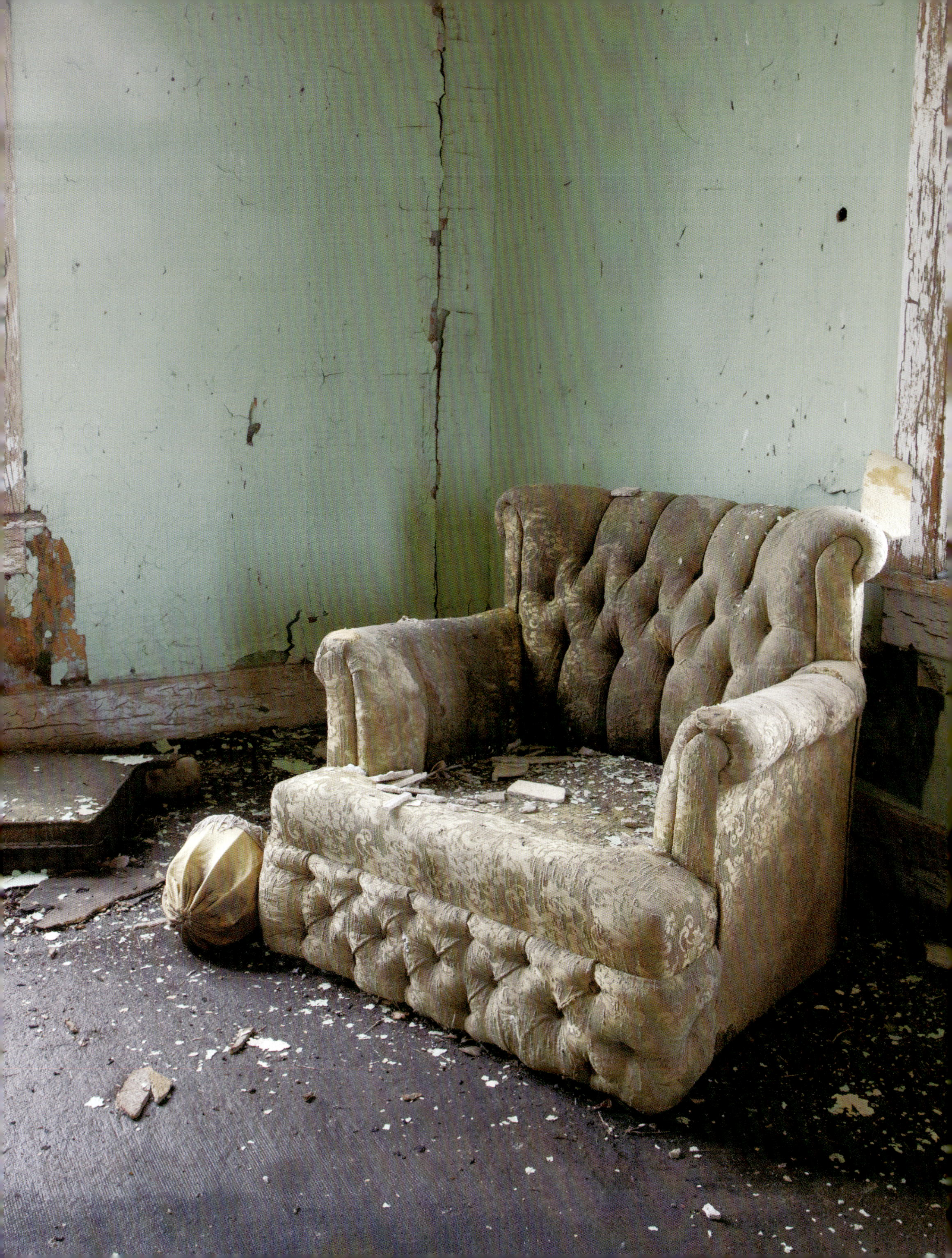

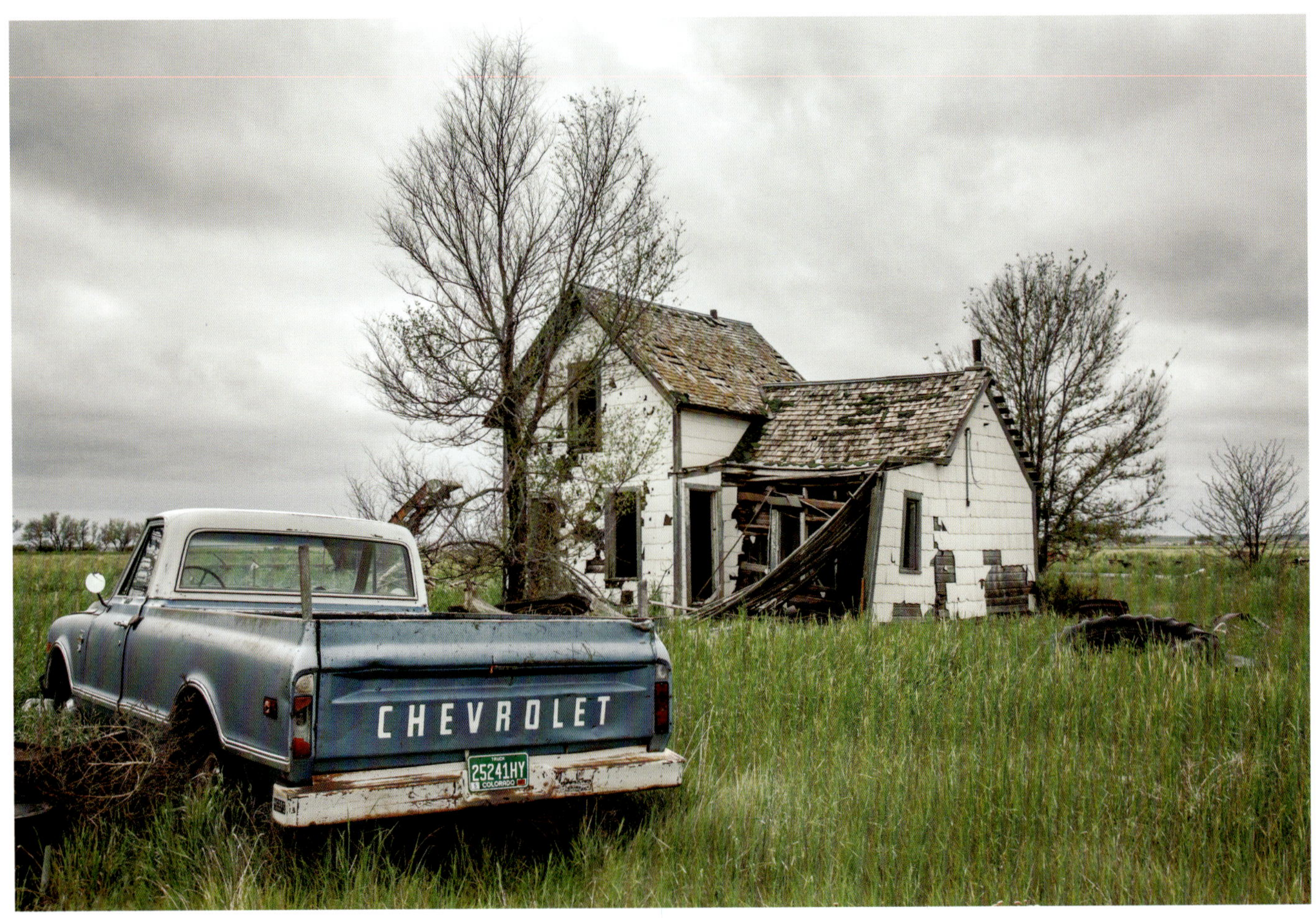

▲

Abandoned homestead west of Fort Morgan, Colorado

Eastern Colorado is one of the most sparsely-populated areas of the United States, with a semi-arid climate yet very cold winters; most small farmers struggle to make a living here.

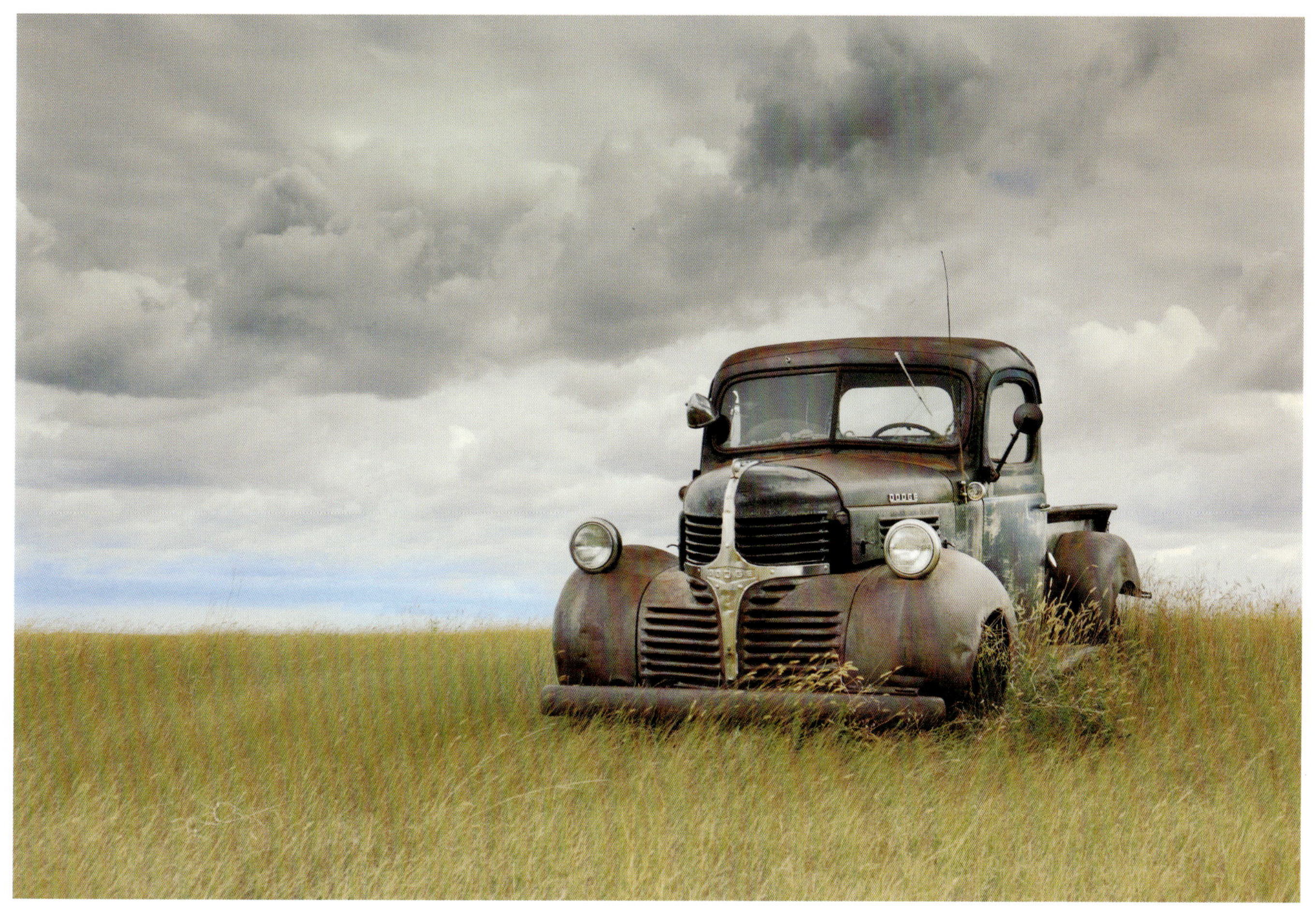

▲

Car in field, Minnesota

When photographing The Plains, we did of course experience a variety of weather, but in order to capture the pathos of this savagely depopulating area, we often preferred to take our photographs under grey skies.

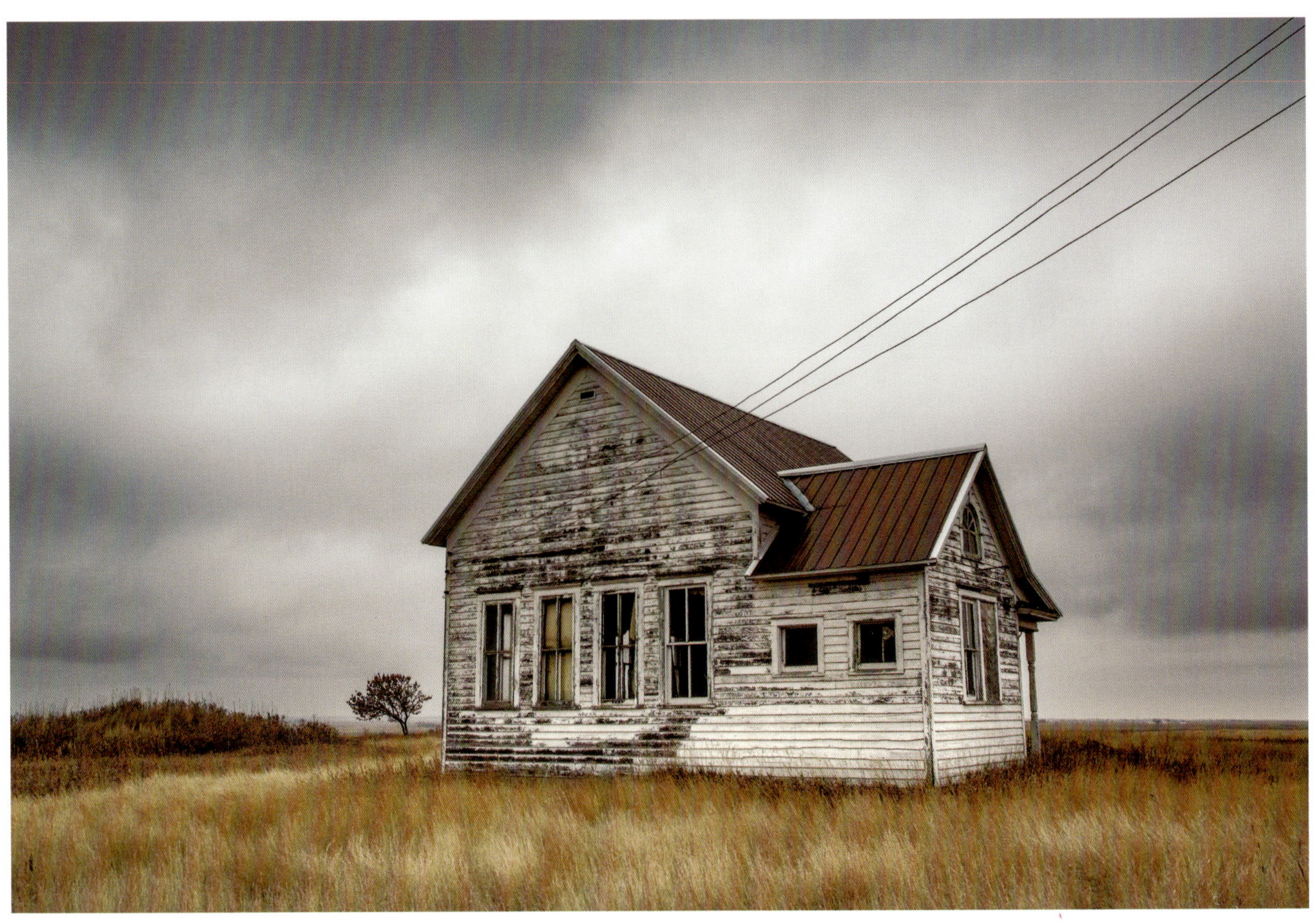

▲

Small school on the prairie

*The majority of schools on the High Plains tend to be single
room or as in this case a two roomed building, and would
service the needs of the children from quite a wide catchment
area. Once abandoned, the local farmer would often use them
as storage for farm machinery.*

▶

Interior, Gurley, Nebraska

*We have seen this house deteriorate over the years and sadly it
has recently burnt down. The peeling paintwork with its limited
palette of colours caught my eye here.*

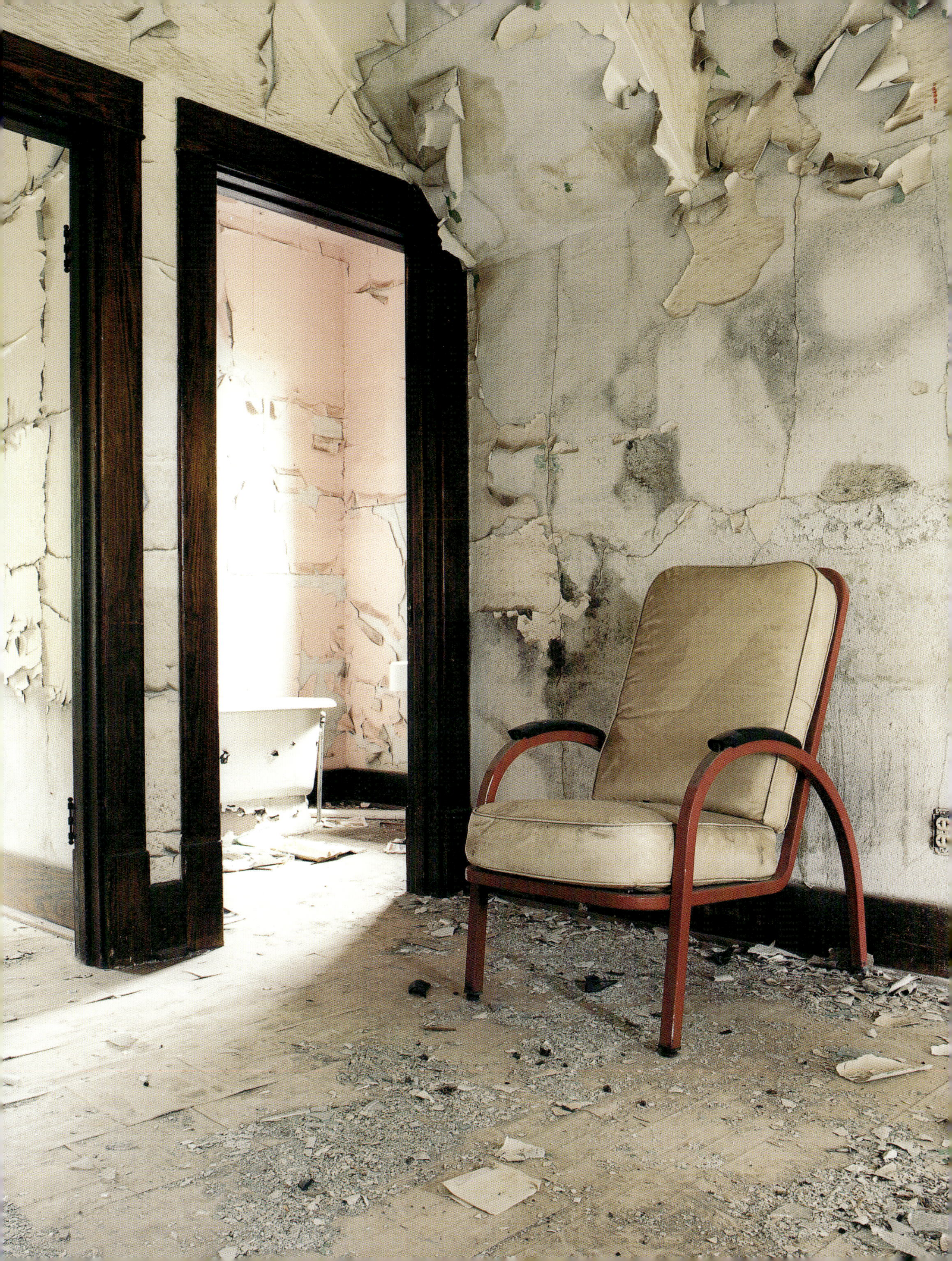

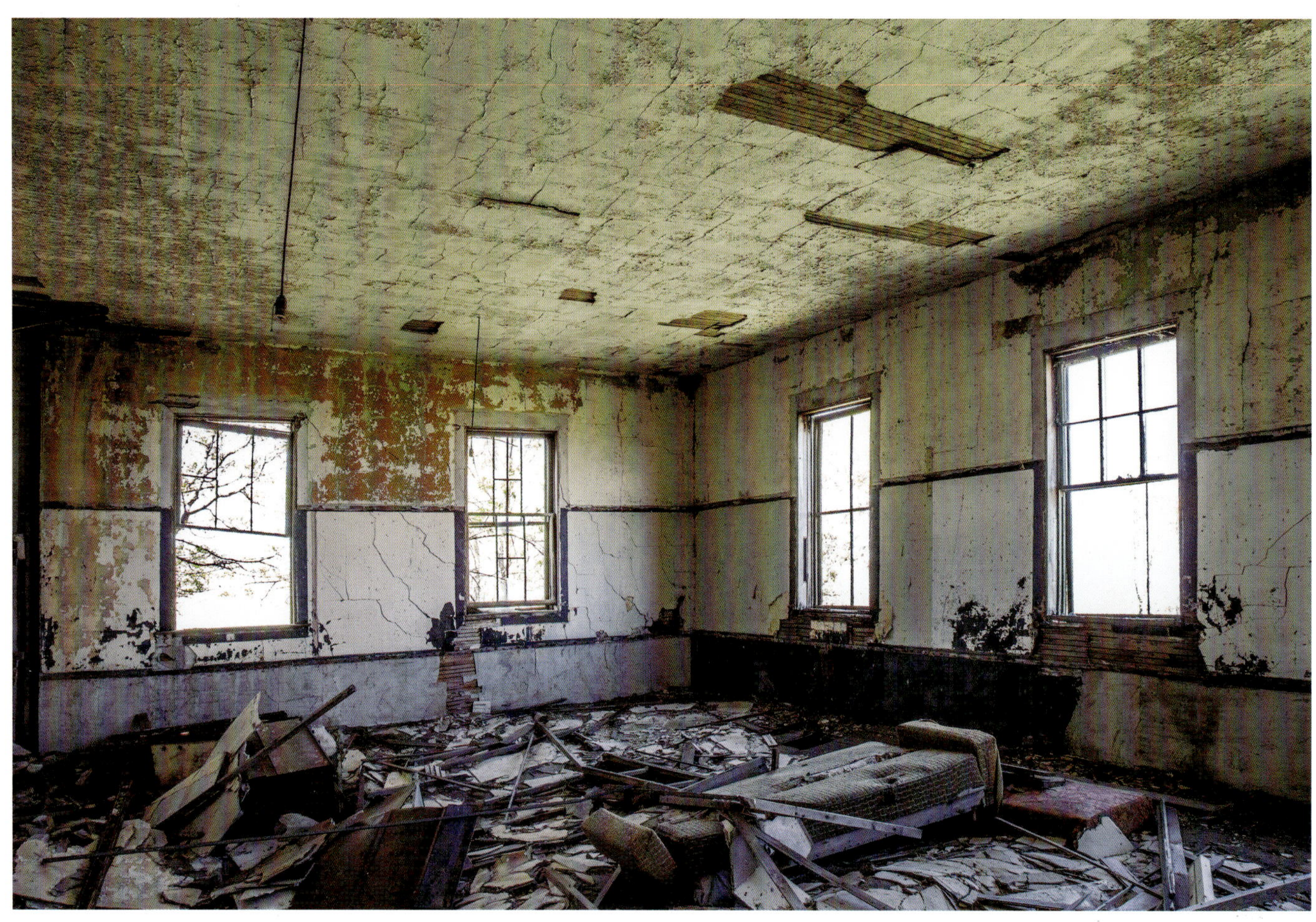

▲

Wrecked school interior

Often buildings such as schools would be used for some other purpose once they were abandoned. I suspect someone had attempted to live here, but then gave up.

▶

Interior with discarded wheelchair

While we rarely found photographs of the past inhabitants, we would often come across objects and artefacts that gave us some insight into the lives of those who once occupied the property. This abandoned wheelchair gave us a small clue.

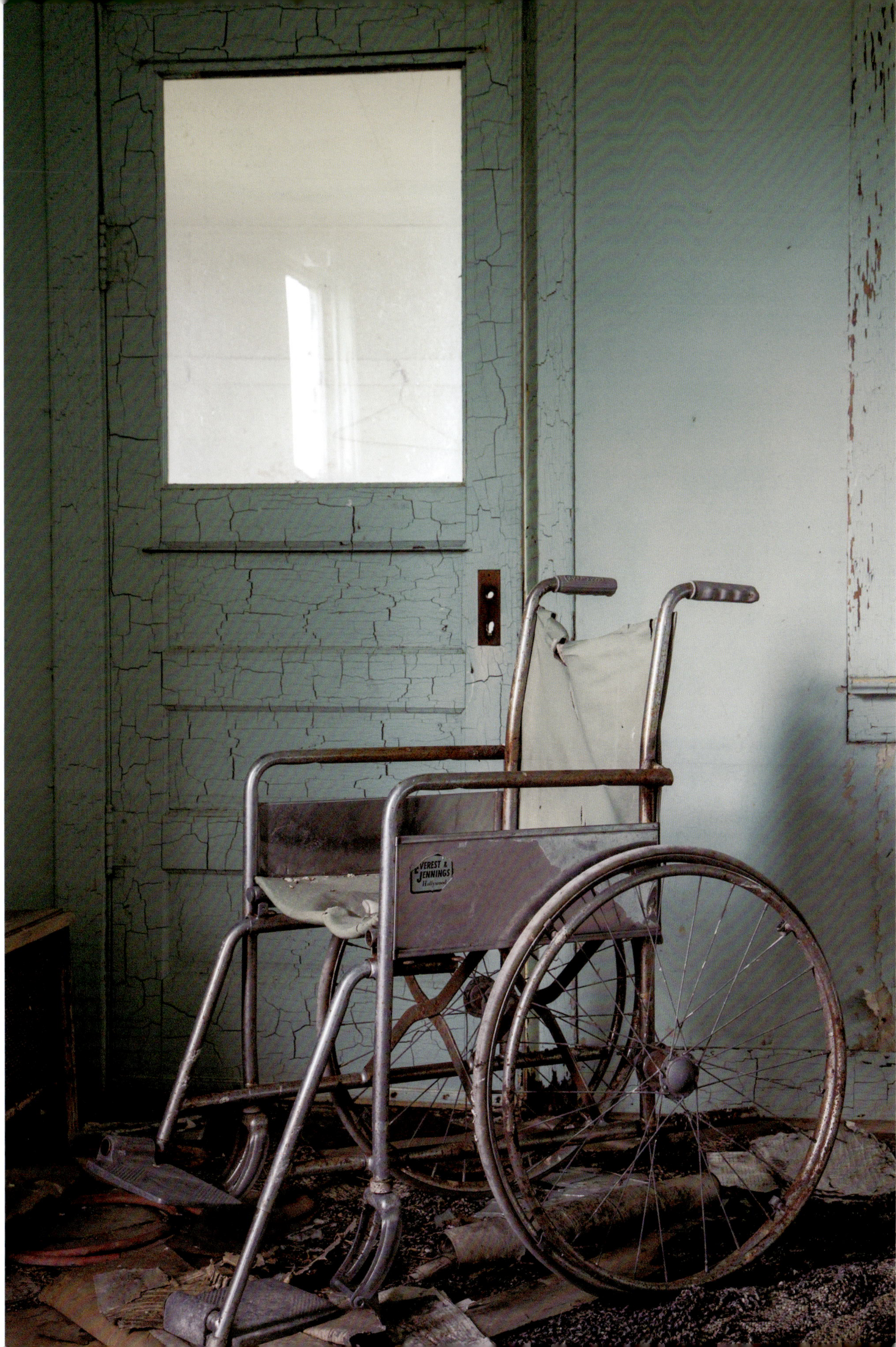

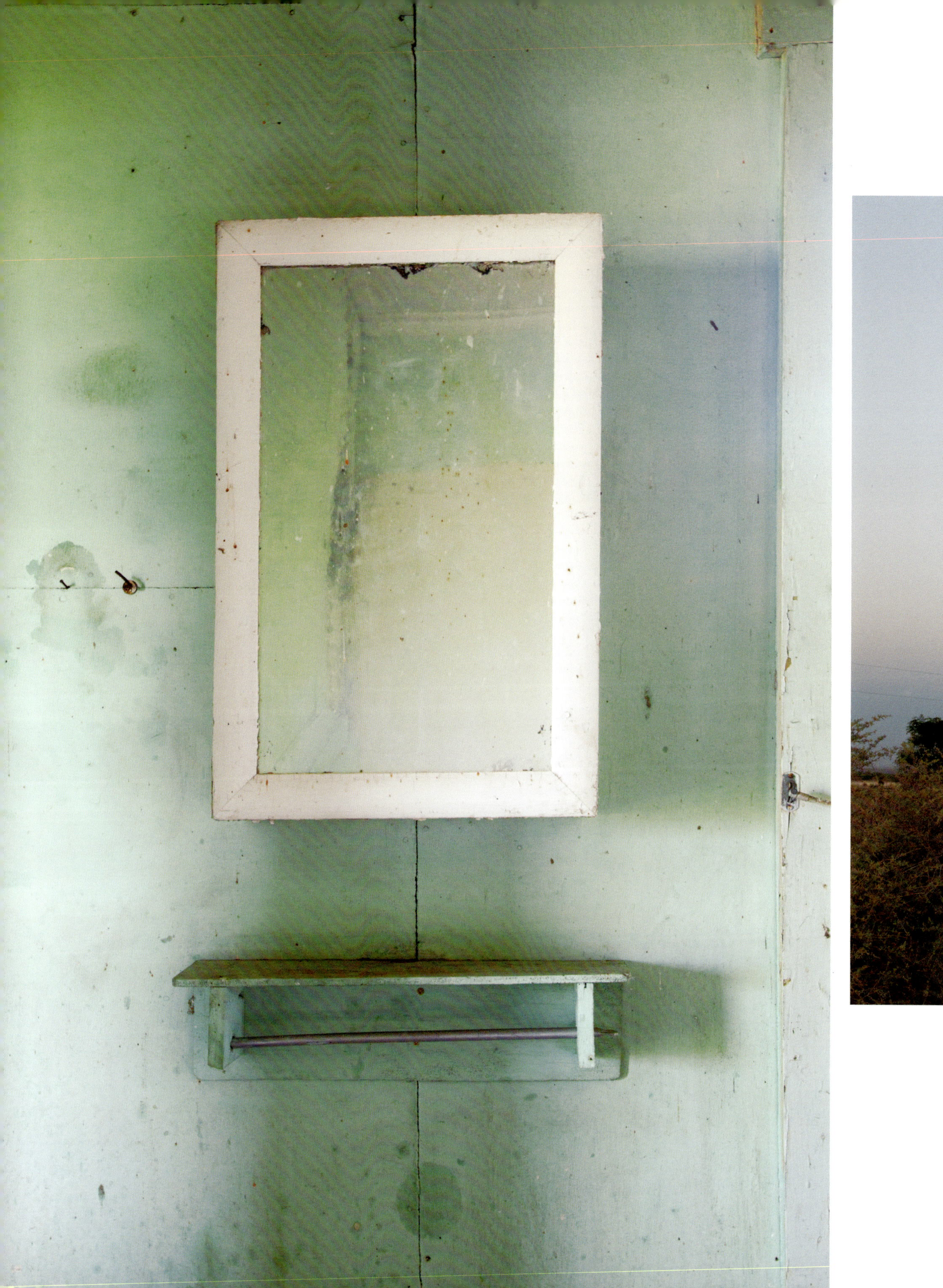

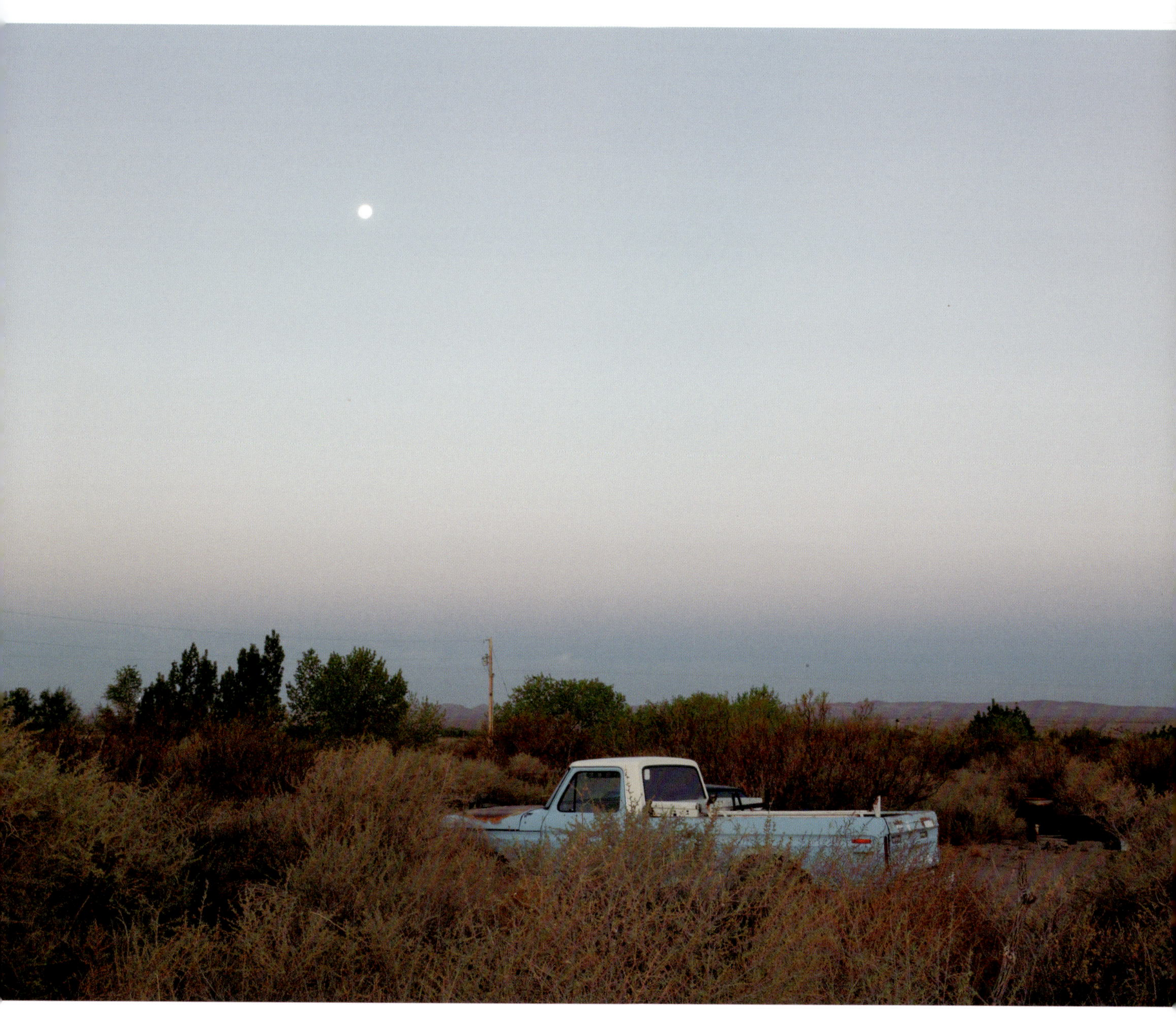

▲

Pickup at dusk, Nebraska

*This blue vehicle, seemingly in the middle of nowhere,
quietly picks up the tones of the sky at twilight.*

◄

Bathroom mirror

*A mirror and, occasionally, the ancient contents
of a bathroom cabinet would be left behind.*

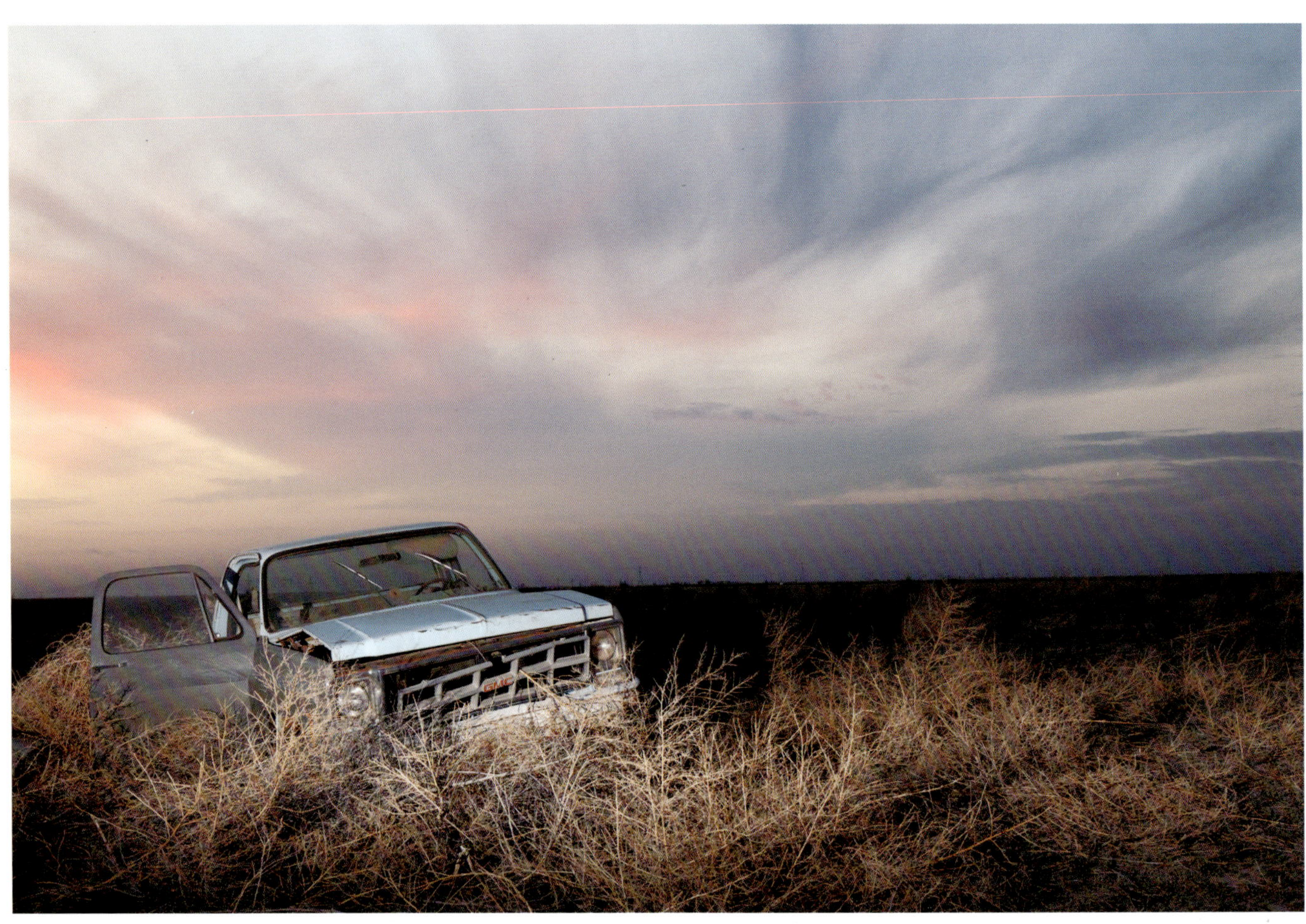

Abandoned on the prairie

While the weather can be extreme on the plains, it does tend to be much drier than the UK, therefore abandoned vehicles are much better preserved. Extra atmosphere was added here by the use of flash, in order to match the power of the dramatic evening sky.

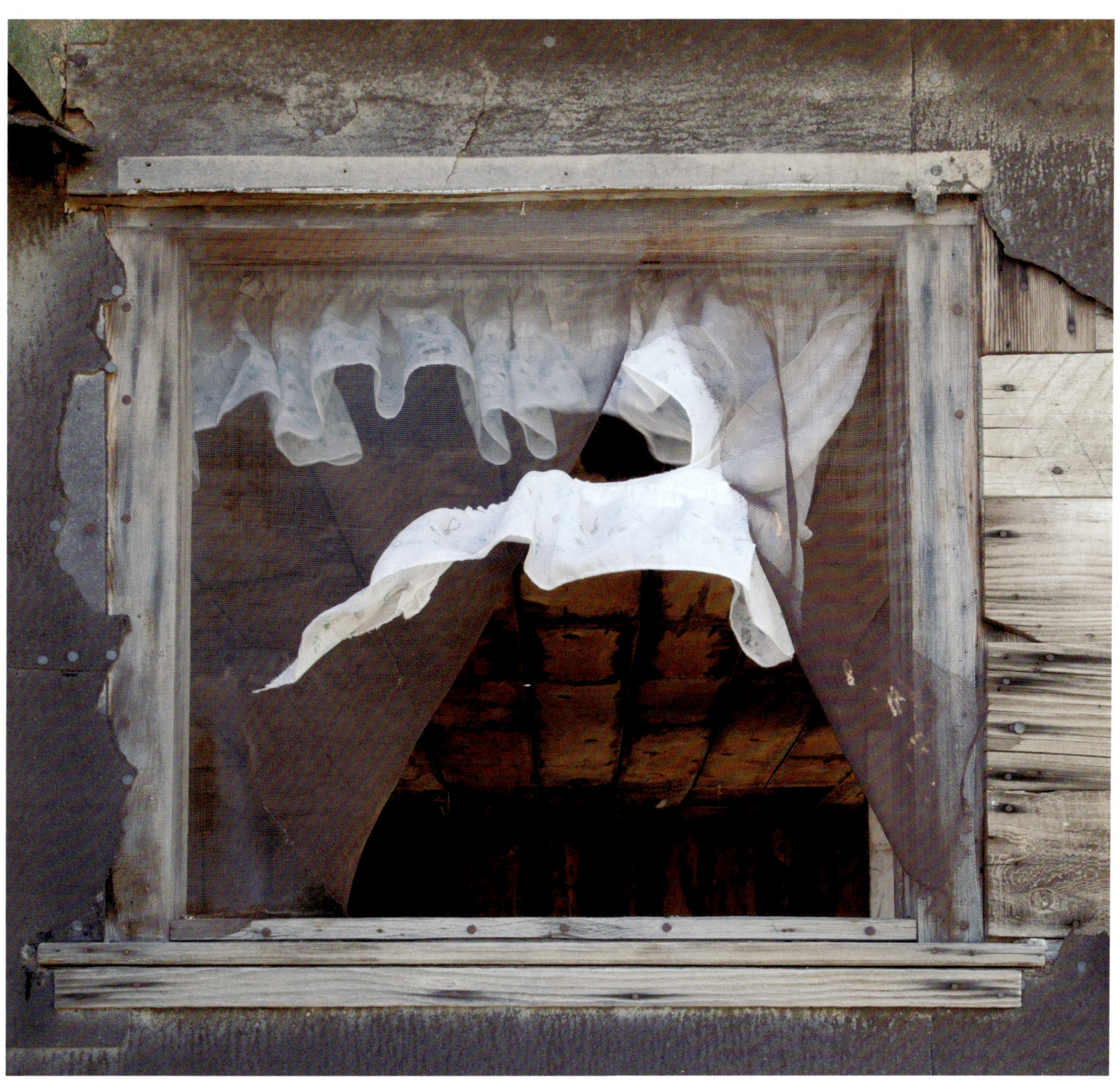

Final curtain

TONY & EVA WOROBIEC

Tony and Eva developed an interest in photography early in their teaching careers and soon joined the RPS; both were awarded a Fellowship from that institution not long afterwards. While initially Tony excelled in black and white and Eva was drawn to colour, both have had their successful panels published by The Journal. They consistently believe that their best work is stimulated by pursuing personal projects, particularly since first travelling to America in 1994.

"Abandoned on the Plains: Fragments of the American Dream" is the fourth publication Tony and Eva have shared and is a sequel to the highly successful *"Ghosts in the Wilderness"*, published by *AAPPL* in 2003. This beautifully printed book earned glowing reviews from The Guardian newspaper, The Independent, The Washington Post and Stern Magazine in Germany and is often referred to as a seminal publication on the depopulating communities of Montana and the Dakotas.

Although Eva and Tony have shared numerous exhibitions together, possibly the most prestigious was when they were invited to show images from their *"Icons of the Highway"* project at The Fox Talbot Museum at Lacock. This body of work was taken from another much praised publication of the same name, which celebrated the disappearing diners, cinemas and motels of small-town America.

Frequent visitors to mainland Europe, Tony and Eva have enjoyed shooting landscape, particularly in Andalusia, and were delighted to have recently been invited to join the esteemed *Landscape Collective* group of photographers.

See more of their work at:

www.tonyworobiec.com
www.evaworobiecphotography.com